D1453293

John Steinbeck
as Propagandist

The University of Alabama Press
Tuscaloosa & London

the Moon Is Down

Goes to War

DONALD V. COERS

designed by
zig zeigler

Library of Congress Cataloging-in-Publication Data

Coers, Donald V., 1941–
    John Steinbeck as propagandist : The moon is down goes to war / Donald V.
Coers.
        p.   cm.
Includes bibliographical references (p.   ) and index.
    ISBN 0-8173-0538-6
    1. Steinbeck, John, 1902–1968. Moon is down. 2. Steinbeck. John, 1902–1968—
Appreciation—Europe. 3. Steinbeck, John, 1902–1968—Political and social
views. 4. World War, 1939–1945—Literature and the war. 5. World War, 1939–
1945—Propaganda. 6. Propaganda, American. I. Title.
PS3537 . T3234M683 1991
813' . 52—dc20   90-26583
                                                            CIP

British Library Cataloguing-in-Publication Data available

FOR MARY JEANNE

Contents

Preface

N EARLY March 1942, a scant three months after Pearl Harbor, John Steinbeck published his play-novel *The Moon Is Down,* igniting in this country the most heated literary debate of the Second World War. He had intended to celebrate the "durability of democracy" with this fablelike tale, in which a small, peace-loving country, rather like Norway, is demoralized after being invaded by a powerful fascist state, rather like Nazi Germany, but recovers from the shock of defeat and occupation to form a promising resistance movement. Steinbeck had been eager to lend his talents to the Allied war effort, and he had hoped that *The Moon Is Down* would boost morale both in his own country and in occupied Europe by proclaiming that free people are inherently stronger than the "herd people" controlled by totalitarian leaders, and that, despite the initial advantage of the militarily mighty dictators, the democracies would eventually win the war.

X I I

Steinbeck's optimism was not widely shared during the dark winter days of 1942, when the Japanese were still advancing in the Pacific and the Germans, having already marched through much of Europe, continued on the offensive in Russia and in North Africa. In fact, his faith seemed dangerously naive to some influential American critics who were convinced that Steinbeck's message was bad propaganda because it made an Allied victory seem inevitable. These critics, who were led by Clifton Fadiman and James Thurber, believed that a superior propagandistic ploy would have been to present the bitter prospect that the war could very easily still be lost. Steinbeck's detractors also objected to his depiction of the Nazilike invaders in his tale. He had done something unusual for a propagandist of this period. He had presented the enemy not as demons but as thoughtful and intelligent human beings committing evil. Steinbeck believed that the customary propagandistic hype would be ineffective among Europeans who were experiencing the occupation firsthand and who would know therefore that not all Germans were monsters. His critics, on the other hand, claimed that those Europeans would be baffled and even demoralized by such "idealized" Nazis.

To be sure, Steinbeck had his defenders during the months in which the debate over *The Moon Is Down* was played out in American journals and popular magazines.

PREFACE

Among them were sympathetic literary critics as well as interested readers and foreign and domestic observers who were confident that Steinbeck's effort would inspire hope and stiffen resolve in occupied Europe. Not until after the war, however, did we know how the novel had actually been received there. Letters written to Steinbeck by former members of the resistance, along with the accounts of several European scholars and writers and the commendations accompanying an award given to Steinbeck by an appreciative Norwegian government in 1946, all suggest that *The Moon Is Down* was indeed popular reading as well as effective propaganda in much of Nazi-occupied Europe.

But during the nearly half century since the end of the war, almost nothing has been added to the record about what actually happened to the novel in countries under German control—about how it was smuggled past the Nazis, translated into various languages, and illegally printed and distributed. Nor have we learned much about why it was popular in occupied countries, or, in fact, about just how popular it actually was. This study attempts to supply the missing details, as vital to our appreciation of Steinbeck the writer as they are to our understanding of propagandistic techniques and of the anti-Nazi resistance in western Europe. Those details are provided mostly through letters and personal interviews of people who were directly involved.

I have incurred numerous debts during my research and writing. The earliest is to the National Endowment for the Humanities Summer Seminar Program, for giving me the opportunity to spend the summer of 1979 at Stanford University attending Ian Watt's seminar "The Historical and Sociological Criticism of Literature." I am grateful to Mr. Watt for his guidance of my major seminar project, later expanded into the present book, and for his comments on the completed manuscript. For early financial support I thank the South Central Modern Languages Association. Its overseas research award defrayed the cost of the European travel necessary for most of my interviews.

For information about Steinbeck's work in government agencies at the time he conceived the idea for *The Moon Is Down*, I am indebted to John Houseman, Geoffrey M. T. Jones, Richard Helms, Archibald MacLeish, Thomas Troy, Kermit Roosevelt, Donald Morris, C. Brooks Peters, Joseph Persico, Norman Cousins, Pascal Covici, Jr., Richard Dunlop, David Schoenbrun, Alan Williams, Theodore White, Charles MacDonald, Richard Sommers, Larry R. Strawderman, and Roberta S. Knapp.

A number of individuals assisted me in locating former members of the resistance and others with first-hand information about the translation, printing, distribution, and reception of *The Moon Is Down* in Nazi-occupied Denmark, Norway, Holland, and France and in wartime Sweden, Switzerland, Italy, and China. I am most appreciative of their time-consuming efforts. They include Per Hasselgärde, Gordon Hølmebakk, Magne Skodvin, Geert Lübberhuizen, Mogens Knudsen, Søren Baggesen, B. Munk Olsen, Jørgen Erik Nielsen, Antonio Carrelli, Giovanna Bernau, G. Debusscher, Henning Gehrs, Henrik Lundbak, Svein Johs Ottesen, Otto Lindhardt, Alan Williams, Charles MacDonald, Jean-Pierre Rosselli, Pierre Rosselli, Ingebjørg Nesheim, Kristin Brudevoll, P. J. Riis, Carl Wandel, A. F. M. van der Ploeg, and a spokesman for the Zhong Hua Book Company of Beijing.

I owe a considerable debt to those who, with invariable kindness, granted interviews or otherwise gave me information vital to this book: Jacques Debû-Bridel, Jørgen Jacobsen, Frits von der Lippe, Bo Beskow, Mrs. John Steinbeck, William Colby, the Zhong Hua Book Company of Beijing, Yvonne Motchane-Desvignes, Ferdinand Sterneberg, Svein Johs Ottesen, Arne Skouen, Chien Gochuen, John Dahl, Gordon Hølmebakk, Mogens Knudsen, Pierre Rosselli, Mogens Staffeldt, Richard Dunlop, Kjell Larsgaard, Larry R. Strawderman, Veit Wyler, Oddvar Aas, Torbjørn Trysnes, Giovanna Bernau, and Piero Cecchini.

For translating foreign newspaper articles, letters, passages from books, and other material, I thank Mary

Gutermuth, Hanna Lewis, Don Stalling, Eva Van Hooser, Henning Gehrs, Henrik Lundbak, and Jørgen Jacobsen.

Several librarians and archivists were especially helpful during the course of my research: Susan Riggs at Stanford; Ellen Dunlap, Ken Craven, and Catherine Henderson at the Harry Ransom Humanities Research Center, The University of Texas at Austin; Erling Grønland at the University of Oslo; Leif H. Rosenstock, Henning Gehrs, and Henrik Lundbak at the Museum of Denmark's Fight for Freedom, 1940–1945; Lotte Hellinga and Anna E. C. Simoni of the British Library; Synnøve Vervik and Hanne Mulelider of Gyldendal Norsk Forlag; Shirley Parotti of the Newton Gresham Library, Sam Houston State University; and the director and staff of the Éditions de Minuit in Paris.

I am grateful to William B. Todd of the University of Texas at Austin and to several of my colleagues at Sam Houston State University who have read various portions of my manuscript and offered useful suggestions: Barbara Tyson, Rob Adams, Paul Ruffin, Hugh Meredith, Eleanor Mitchell, and my chairman, James Goodwin. Tetsumaro Hayashi of the Steinbeck Society of America at Ball State University also offered constructive suggestions. Special credit is due Gary Bell, Don Stalling, and my wife, Mary Jeanne, for their encouragement throughout the course of my research and

PREFACE

writing as well as for careful commentary on the entire manuscript. I also express my appreciation to Elaine Steinbeck for her help and gracious support.

I must acknowledge warmly the invaluable advice and the many courtesies of Acquisitions Editor Nicole Mitchell and the staff of The University of Alabama Press, the technical assistance of Jeanne Coers, who typed the final manuscript, and of Westin McCoy, Laura Howey, and Henry Howey, who helped prepare the final version, and the special help extended by Hank Conaway, Richard Allen, Ralph Cooley, Vikár László, Virginia Irvin, and Friedel Werner.

Finally, I give heartfelt thanks to my wife Mary Jeanne, my daughter Jeanne, and my son John, for their interest, support, and cheerful forbearance.

1

Publication
and American
Reception

Y THE TIME the Nazis launched their invasions into western Europe in the spring of 1940, John Steinbeck had reached the peak of his career. After the extraordinary critical and commercial success of *The Grapes of Wrath* a year earlier, crowning a half decade of achievement which saw the publication of *Tortilla Flat* (1935), *In Dubious Battle* (1936), *Of Mice and Men* (1937), and *The Long Valley* (1938), Steinbeck stood in the ranks of such living American literary luminaries as Ernest Hemingway, F. Scott Fitzgerald, William Faulkner, and Sinclair Lewis. In March and April 1940, Steinbeck sought respite from the clamor of "damnable popularity" when he and his close friend Ed Ricketts, a marine biologist, sailed into the Gulf of California on a specimen-collecting expedition that would furnish material for *Sea of Cortez* (1941), a scientific and philosophical manifesto of Steinbeck's "tide-pool" theory of life.

In May, Steinbeck was in Mexico writing the screen-play for a motion picture about life in an Indian village. There he became troubled about what he perceived as an inadequate U.S. response to Nazi Bund activities in Latin America. His agitation being fed by news of German military victories at the time, Steinbeck wrote about his fears to an uncle, Joseph Hamilton, then working for the Works Progress Administration in Washington, D.C. "The Germans have absolutely outclassed the Allies in propaganda. If it continues, they will completely win Central and South America away from the United States." He went on to propose that a propaganda office be established which would use "radio and motion pictures . . . to get this side of the world together."[1]

On 24 June, shortly after his return from Mexico and only two days after France had signed an armistice with Germany, Steinbeck wrote to President Roosevelt, conveying his feelings about shortcomings in American propaganda in the Western Hemisphere and offering to speak with the president about the problem.

> For some time I have been making a little moving picture in Mexico. In this line I have covered a great deal of country and had conversations with many people of many factions.
>
> In the light of this experience and against a background of the international situation, I am forced to the conclusion that a crisis in the Western Hemi-

sphere is imminent, and is to be met only by an immediate, controlled, considered, and directed method and policy.

It is probable that you have considered this situation in all its facets. However, if my observation can be of any use to you, I shall be very glad to speak with you for I am sure that this problem is one of the most important to be faced by the nation.[2]

Accompanying Steinbeck's letter when it arrived at Roosevelt's desk was a note signed by James Rowe, Jr., then special White House assistant to the president, suggesting that Steinbeck "probably has no better information than any other sensitive and intelligent layman who has spent time in Mexico." A handwritten addendum, however, was more positive. "Archie [Archibald] MacLeish [the poet, then librarian of Congress] says he thinks you would be interested in talking with him. He is the author of *The Grapes of Wrath.*" Roosevelt asked his secretary, General Marvin ("Pa") Watson, to schedule a twenty-minute meeting with Steinbeck for 26 June.[3]

Apparently, whatever specific ideas Steinbeck presented in the White House during that meeting were not adopted by the president, nor would it be the only time Steinbeck's ideas for aiding the U.S. war effort would be ignored or rejected. Just after Pearl Harbor, Steinbeck and Ed Ricketts offered the Navy Department copies of zoological surveys conducted by Japanese scientists among the Pacific islands mandated to Japan after World War I and subsequently closed to foreigners. Steinbeck and Ricketts had received the material, with its militarily vital data on weather, currents, reefs, winds, coastlines, and tidal ranges, from American universities, where it had been sent before the war by the conscientious scientists who had compiled it. The Navy Department never examined the material.[4] On another occasion, Steinbeck and one of his scientist friends, Dr. M. H. Knisely, presented Roosevelt with a plan to undermine the economy of the Third Reich by flooding Germany with counterfeit money. The president seemed to like the idea, but Secretary of the Treasury Henry Morgenthau and the British ambassador, Lord Halifax, strongly disapproved, and the scheme was dropped.[5]

Twenty years after the war ended, Steinbeck joked about his rejected offers. In one of a series of articles he wrote for *Weekend with Newsday,* he says that, like Bernard Baruch, he was an adviser to presidents. "No one knows how much of Mr. Baruch's advice the Presidents took. With me it is easier. I can find no evidence that they ever took any of it."[6]

The author did, however, have some successes in his efforts to lend his talents to the fight against fascism. During the early years of the war, he was assigned to various government jobs, mainly in the intelligence and information agencies hastily created between 1940 and

1942. Over two decades later, Steinbeck recalled his wartime government service in a brief article in the *Book Week* section of the New York Sunday *Herald Tribune.* "I worked for the Air Force, the Writers' War Board, the Office of War Information and even for the O.S.S. [Office of Strategic Services]. I wrote everything— speeches, essays, stories, plays, broadcasts, a whole volume about the training of bomber crews, everything I could devise or that was suggested to me and there were dozens of writers doing the same thing."[7]

It was his association with one of those agencies— Steinbeck himself said it was the Office of War Information—which brought him into contact with refugees from countries overrun by the Germans and gave him the idea of writing a fictional account of the traumas of Nazi occupation. He became particularly fascinated with stories about the resistance organizations in the homelands of the refugees—those underground "secret armies" which "refused to admit defeat even when Germans patrolled their streets." He had soon heard enough about the patriotic responses to occupation in the various countries to conclude that "while they differed in some degree with national psychologies," they had much in common.

At the time of the invasion there had been confusion; in some of the nations there were secret Nazi parties, there were spies and turncoats. [The Norwegian Nazi, Vidkun] Quisling has left his name as a synonym for traitor. Then there were collaborators, some moved by fear and others simply for advancement and profit. Finally there were the restrictive measures of the Germans, their harsh demands and savage punishments. All of these factors had to be correlated and understood before an underground movement could form and begin to take action.[8]

By September 1941 Steinbeck, eager to encourage the resistance in the victim nations, had decided to correlate in a work of fiction what he had learned about the psychological effects of enemy occupation upon the populace of conquered nations.[9] Because he "did not believe people are very different in essentials," he originally set his story in America.

> I wrote my fictional account about a medium-sized American town with its countryside of a kind I knew well. There would be collaborators certainly. Don't forget the Bund meetings in our cities, the pro-German broadcasts before the war and the kind of man who loves any success: "Mussolini made the trains run on time." "Hitler saved Germany from communism." It was not beyond reason that our town would have its cowards, its citizens who sold out for profit. But under this, I did and do believe, would be the hard core that could not be defeated. And so I wrote

my account basing its fiction on facts extracted from towns already under the Nazi heel.[10]

The organization for which Steinbeck was working (he does not say which one it was) when he submitted his "fictional account" rejected his story because it was not true (the United States had not been occupied) and because postulating an American defeat might be demoralizing. While Steinbeck disagreed with the reasons for the bureaucratic disapproval, he was willing to abandon his story. His friends from Norwegian, Danish, French, and Czech resistance groups who had first encouraged his project were less acquiescent. They urged him to circumvent the official objections simply by shifting the setting to that of an occupied country. No one had yet written such an account of the experience of Nazi occupation, and Steinbeck's friends were certain that his story would boost morale in their homelands. Steinbeck followed their advice and made the necessary revisions. "I placed the story in an unnamed country, cold and stern like Norway, cunning and implacable like Denmark, reasonable like France. The names of people in the book I made as international as I could. I did not even call the Germans Germans but simply invaders. I named the book 'The Moon Is Down' from a line in 'Macbeth' and sent it to press."[11]

Steinbeck faced one final problem before *The Moon Is Down* was ready for his publisher. He had dictated his revised version to a court reporter he had hired—a large, "very severe-looking" woman who seemed to become more hostile day by day as they worked. After he discovered that she was making significant changes of her own—including leaving out entire passages—Steinbeck fired her. Later he learned that she had been attending local chapter meetings of the German-American Bund, an ostensible friendship society which was in fact little more than an outlet for Nazi propaganda.[12]

One of several cloudy details in accounts of how Steinbeck came to write *The Moon Is Down* is obviously the result of a minor lapse in the author's memory about the organization with which he was associated when he conceived and composed his work. According to Steinbeck, he was serving in the Office of War Information when he met the refugees who first interested him in writing about the effects of occupation. But the OWI was not established until 13 June 1942—three months after the publication of the novel version of *The Moon Is Down* and six months after Steinbeck wrote his old friend and attorney Webster F. (Toby) Street that the play version would be ready for production within a week.[13] According to Steinbeck biographer Jackson Benson, the author was assigned at the time to the office of Coordinator of Information (later the Office of Strategic Services). Within that office, Steinbeck served in the unit of Robert Sherwood, Pulitizer-Prize-winning playwright. Sherwood had staffed his unit, the Foreign Information Service (FIS), with well-known writers and journalists. Steinbeck did in fact attend a meeting of a group within the FIS in October 1941 to discuss future FIS activities.[14]

More curious than Steinbeck's understandable failure of memory about an organization for which he had worked briefly some twenty years earlier is his failure ever to confirm an often-cited claim about the composition of *The Moon Is Down* made in 1943 by his friend Lewis Gannett, whose wife Ruth, had drawn the illustrations for *Tortilla Flat*. In his introduction to *The Portable Steinbeck,* Gannett, a longtime book critic for the *New York Herald Tribune,* said that "*The Moon Is Down* actually grew out of a serious discussion with Colonel William J. Donovan of the Office of Strategic Services on techniques for aiding resistance movements in the occupied countries of German-held Europe."[15] Unfortunately, Gannett, who died in 1966, gave no source for his claim.[16] What we know about Donovan and the intelligence operations he led, however, suggests that he would have welcomed Steinbeck's help.

A brilliant and successful New York lawyer, Colonel Donovan was a hero of the First World War whose

awards included the Congressional Medal of Honor, the
Distinguished Service Medal, and the Distinguished Service Cross. At the time of Steinbeck's government service, Donovan was the prime figure in the development
of the first central intelligence organizations in this country, first as head of the Office of Coordinator of Information (COI), which Roosevelt approved on 11 July
1941, and then as director of the Office of Strategic
Services (OSS), created on 13 June 1942. In both capaci-
ties Donovan proved an open-minded and occasionally
unorthodox administrator who, despite his political
conservatism, was willing to use outré people and ideas if
they suited his purposes. In the COI and later in the
OSS, consequently, one found "Bolsheviks among the
bluebloods" and writers and artists among military men
and bureaucrats. Those whose services Donovan enlisted included poet Archibald MacLeish, authors Ed-
ward Taylor and Douglas Miller, President Roosevelt's
son James, Supreme Court Justice Felix Frankfurter's
daughter Estelle, foreign editor of the *New York Herald
Tribune* Joseph Barnes, and Hollywood producers
Merian C. Cooper, best remembered for *King Kong*, and
John Ford, who had recently done the film version of
The Grapes of Wrath.[17]

Clearly, Donovan was the kind of man who would
have been interested in exchanging ideas with a first-rate
writer like John Steinbeck. Donovan had always recog-

nized the importance of morale—his first assignment as a special presidential envoy for Roosevelt in 1940, in fact, was to gauge the public spirit and general readiness for war in England. Thus, he might have been especially receptive to a discussion with the author of *The Grapes of Wrath* about a work of fiction designed to raise the spirits of those whose countries were occupied by a power which most Americans already perceived as an enemy.

Whatever the uncertainties about the genesis of *The Moon Is Down,* there is no doubt about the vehemence of the controversy which greeted the publication of the work itself. The Viking Press brought out the novel version in early March 1942, and within days the most heated literary debate in this country during the Second World War was underway. Before the brouhaha subsided nearly a year after it began, it had engaged not only famed critics but a cross-section of the American and European public as well.

The first extensive review of *The Moon Is Down* was highly favorable. In the *New York Times* for 6 March 1942, John Chamberlain praised the universality of Steinbeck's treatment as well as his "exact perception of how a free people must react to an attempt to enforce slavery upon it" and pronounced *The Moon Is Down* "the most memorable fiction to have come out of this war."[18] The critics' war began the next day when Clifton Fadiman, writing in the *New Yorker,* lambasted the novel as deceptive in literary form (it was not a novel at all but a melodramatic play disguised as a novel) and bad propaganda as well (it rested on the dangerously naive assumption that an Allied victory was inevitable because good always triumphs over evil). "It is becoming increasingly clear," said Fadiman, "that [Steinbeck's] form of spiritual patriotism is not only not enough but may even impede the war effort, because it fills us with a specious satisfaction...it seduces us to rest on the oars of our own moral superiority.[19]

On 8 March R. L. Duffus of the *New York Times Book Review* dismissed the question of genre by proclaiming that "a novel must probably be defined as any story between covers" and praised *The Moon Is Down* as a remarkable novel, "so strong, so simple, so true, so dramatic in its values."[20] A review by John Gunther appearing on the same day in the *New York Herald Tribune Books* commended the "wonderful effects" Steinbeck achieves "by making the German commander, Colonel Lanser, a sympathetically conceived human being," even though the novel "is almost maddeningly fair-minded to the Germans." He cited *The Moon Is Down* as "a miraculous example of the way a great storyteller can clarify in a work of art the overwhelmingly dominant issue of the time."[21] *Time* magazine for 9 March decided the novel was "great propaganda" because of its "certainty of viewpoint that does not admit the possibility of final military defeat because it does not admit the possibility of moral defeat."[22] On 16 March James Thurber, writing in the *New Republic*, supported Clifton Fadiman's arguments, maintaining that Steinbeck's very title was likely to get him "into soft and dreamy trouble" and concluding that "a title like 'Guts in the Mud' would have produced a more convincing reality." Thurber also criticized the "German" officers as unrealistic, sarcastically suggesting that the story "will make a very pretty movie," although he wondered "what the people of Poland would make of it all."[23]

After the initial exchanges by the earliest reviewers, response from other critics and the public alike was fast in coming and often ferocious in tone. On 30 March the *New Republic* announced it was publishing letters about the merits of *The Moon Is Down* in its correspondence departments. It also noted that one reason for the bitterness of the controversy so far was that "those who like or dislike the book are often judging it by different standards," but it added editorially that "no one has ever heard of such Hamlet-like Nazis as Mr. Steinbeck portrays, except as exceedingly rare individual exceptions."[24]

The first letter in the *New Republic*'s forum on 30 March was written by Marshall A. Best. Best defended *The Moon Is Down* against Thurber's attack by claiming that "three good writers—who know Europe at least as well as Thurber does" had recommended that the novel be translated and distributed in occupied countries, and by suggesting that the country is not well served by "parlor intellectuals" and "owls in the attic."[25] Directly below Best's letter was Thurber's response to it. Pointing out that Mr. Best was the managing editor of the Viking Press (publishers of *The Moon Is Down*), Thurber declared himself "approximately as deeply moved [by Best's defense] as [he] would be by the tears of a real-estate agent."[26] A third letter, signed simply "Polish Refugee," supported Thurber's view that Steinbeck's Nazis are unrealistic by observing that they are indeed "so exceptional that they ought not to be used in a literary work as representatives of the German army" and by decrying "such distorted, honeyed visions of our tortured life as the one in Mr. Steinbeck's novel."[27]

Clifton Fadiman fired off his second salvo in the 4 April edition of the *New Yorker*. After explaining that "several low-boiling-point readers have written in to condemn my deficient enthusiasm for John Steinbeck's 'The Moon Is Down,'" Fadiman claimed that even after rereading it, he still could not see it "as anything more than brilliantly manipulated melodrama, the effect of whose propaganda is at least debatable." Although he professed himself to be "a veteran Steinbeck admirer" who was certain that Steinbeck was "as sincere an anti-Fascist as any man alive," Fadiman simply could not accept the "fairy-tale atmosphere" surrounding the resistance put up by the citizens of the fictional invaded country.[28]

Early responses to *The Moon Is Down* from foreigners proved to be as mixed as those from home-grown critics. Writing in the *New Republic* for 13 April, Frank G. Nelson, an American guest professor who had spent seven months as a prisoner of the Gestapo in Norway, described Steinbeck's "account of what happened to [the Norwegians'] souls" as "the truest picture I have yet found of both Germans and Norwegians under the occupation of Norway."[29] Nelson's assessment drew a partial endorsement on 4 May in the same magazine from Hans Olav, counselor of the Royal Norwegian Legation in Washington, D.C. Olav wrote that while Norwegians with whom he had spoken were "highly impressed with [Steinbeck's] almost uncanny analysis of the moods of unarmed resistance against the Nazis in Norway," they believed that "his characterization of the Germans *per se*" was "wide of the mark," and regretted that Steinbeck "did not dip his pen in the vitriolic inkstand of, let us say, 'The Grapes of Wrath' and paint a picture of the 'conquerers' as they really are."[30]

Taking a less generous stand on a similar matter, the Belgian Information Center in New York rendered, around the end of April, a "bill of complaints against that part of 'The Moon is Down' in which the Nazi commander relates his experiences in Belgium in the first World War." The Belgian agency maintained that the commander's story of "a little old woman in Brussels who killed twelve men with a long black hatpin" was the kind of fabrication that provided an excuse for German atrocities at the time and suggested that although Steinbeck's motives were good, he had done "a disservice to the Belgian reputation for dignity and fair play."[31]

An even shriller note in the critics' exchange was sounded by Lewis Gannett on 4 May, when he declared in the *New York Herald Tribune* that "'The New Republic,' seconded by Clifton Fadiman in 'The New Yorker,' has been conducting a totalitarian crusade against John Steinbeck's 'The Moon Is Down,' led, of all people, by that most civilized of American satirists, James Thurber." Gannett expressed alarm at "the book-burning flavor" of the movement and defended Steinbeck's portrayal of Colonel Lanser as a decent and intelligent human being by suggesting that such men "are more dangerous than the undoubting Nazis" because they are "betrayers of intelligence."[32] The *New Republic* for 18 May returned to the issue once again, announcing that, because the din over *The Moon Is Down* had developed "into all-out warfare on the literary front," the factions had been divided into the Blue, or anti-Steinbeck, forces (led by Clifton Fadiman) and the

Green, or pro-Steinbeck, forces (led by John Chamberlain).

Editorially dismissing Lewis Gannett's accusations as "triumphant and total nonsense," the *New Republic* took a careful stand on two of the most frequently raised points of dispute. It argued that Steinbeck was right to depict some of the Nazis as likable, but that he was wrong to portray them all that way, and decided that insofar as artistic merits were concerned, the novel is unsuccessful because Steinbeck "does not know his people or his background, and the result is that the literary emotion never becomes quite real. The characters make admirable speeches, but they do not talk like human beings."[33]

Because the novel preceded the dramatic version of *The Moon Is Down,* it drew most of the criticism. Nevertheless, the play stirred some controversy of its own. Herman Shumlin, the theatrical producer who had acquired an option on the play even before Steinbeck had finished it, decided later that "he did not care for its politics," so the rights went to Oscar Serlin (best known as the producer of *Life with Father*).[34]

Serlin's production of *The Moon Is Down* opened on Broadway early in April 1942. Reviews were as mixed as those for the novel (although not as numerous), but both novel and play were enthusiastically received by the

American public. According to *Life* magazine, they were "trumpeted louder than any literary event of the season."[35] (Prepublication sales of the novel version had surpassed those of *The Grapes of Wrath* two to one, and this lead continued for several weeks.)[36] The dramatic production played to packed houses for several months.[37] Warren French has noted that the play garnered two votes for the New York Critics' Circle award for best play of 1942–43, although, as it turned out, no award was given for that season.[38]

After its run on Broadway, *The Moon Is Down* was sold to Twentieth Century–Fox for what was then a phenomenal $300,000. Directed by Irving Pichel, with a screenplay by Nunnally Johnson, the film version appeared in March 1943, one year after the publication of the novel. Like the novel and the play, the movie was popular with the general public, although it also received mixed reviews. According to Joseph R. Millichap in *Steinbeck and Film*, "The propagandistic emphasis in both the novel and the play versions of *The Moon Is Down* is escalated in the film adaptation."[39] Notwithstanding what Millichap perceived as a greater propagandistic emphasis, however, the OWI (the same organization Steinbeck erroneously recalled being associated with when he composed *The Moon Is Down*) had, by the time the movie version appeared, become disturbed by Hollywood's frequent stereotyping of Germans and

Japanese as heel-clicking Huns and slant-eyed sadists. In 1943 the OWI commended a number of what it regarded as sophisticated movies which treated the enemy as a serious threat to basic institutions. Among them was the film adaptation of *The Moon Is Down*.[40]

Despite the general popular and commercial success of *The Moon Is Down* in the United States, and even though the number of critics who applauded the work was at the very least roughly equal to the number of those who denounced it, Steinbeck was stunned by the kinds of attacks spearheaded by Thurber and Fadiman. Thurber's review in the *New Republic* was especially galling. According to Jackson Benson, the problem was his attitude.

> He is so certain and so terribly self-righteous. A book review is not just a book announcement or public evaluation; it is also very often a public trial of the author's worth, professional and sometimes personal, and it is a letter from critic to writer. Thurber takes great pleasure in holding up Steinbeck's book to public ridicule, mocking it as only Thurber can mock, and then sending a letter to the author saying, in effect, "You silly bastard."[41]

The Grapes of Wrath had established Steinbeck as one of the three or four best-known writers in the world. He had been hailed for his enlightened and humane political views as well as for his skill as a writer. To a generation of liberal artists and intellectuals committed to the notion that art should serve social progress, Steinbeck had emerged as the preeminent proletarian novelist of his day. Suddenly the publication of his first novel since *The Grapes of Wrath* brought criticism which questioned not only his skill as a writer but also—and far worse—his credentials as an antifascist, his political instincts, and his very patriotism. Over ten years later, in October 1953, Steinbeck referred to the affair in an essay entitled "My Short Novels." His sarcastic reference after so many years to those who had attacked *The Moon Is Down* shortly after its publication (chiefly Thurber and Fadiman) reveals how deeply he had been wounded by their attacks.

> The war came on, and I wrote *The Moon Is Down* as a kind of celebration of the durability of democracy. I couldn't conceive that the book would be denounced. I had written of Germans as men, not supermen, and this was considered a very weak attitude to take. I couldn't make much sense out of this, and it seems absurd now that we know the Germans were men, and thus fallible, even defeatable. It was said that I didn't know anything about war, and this was perfectly true, though how Park Avenue commandos found me out I can't conceive.[42]

AMERICAN RECEPTION

A full decade after that comment, Steinbeck described once more his earlier astonishment when *The Moon Is Down* was "violently, almost hysterically, attacked by several powerful critics as being defeatist, unreal, complacent and next door to treasonable." This time he referred directly to his injured pride. "I must admit that my feelings were hurt by these attacks because I had thought I was doing a good and a patriotic thing."[43]

The criticism leveled against *The Moon Is Down* as literature never bothered Steinbeck. In fact, he actually agreed with some of it. On 10 August 1942 he sent Webster Street some reviews of the Broadway production of *The Moon Is Down*, noting that "they are almost uniformly bad" and "almost uniformly right."[44] War correspondent Quentin Reynolds tells of an incident which occurred in Algiers in September 1943, when Reynolds introduced Steinbeck, then a correspondent himself for the *New York Herald Tribune*, to Lieutenant Douglas Fairbanks, Jr., and Lieutenant Commander John Kramer. After ascertaining that the man he had just met was John Steinbeck the writer, Kramer told him coldly that he thought *The Moon Is Down* was a lousy play. Steinbeck laughed, shook hands with Kramer, and told him he was glad to find someone who agreed with him. "I never liked it. It didn't play well. No, it was a bad play."[45]

But Steinbeck never forgot the charge that his book would actually harm the very cause he had intended it to serve—nor, it would seem, did he ever forgive those who made such a charge. According to his widow, he "always resented bitterly" the American critics' attitude.[46] Nevertheless Steinbeck could feel vindicated when only a year and a half after the war ended, the king of Norway decorated him for his contribution, through *The Moon Is Down*, to the Norwegian war effort. During the 1950s and 1960s Steinbeck occasionally received from grateful Europeans testimonials about the effectiveness as propaganda of *The Moon Is Down* in countries that had been overrun by the Nazis. In 1957 a former member of the Italian underground told him that illegal mimeographed copies of the novel were passed around by the resistance;[47] in 1963 a friend in Denmark sent him a battered copy of the clandestine edition circulated throughout that country during the occupation;[48] and Elaine Steinbeck remembers people telling her husband that they had seen underground copies during the war—or had actually helped to publish it.[49]

Still John Steinbeck never knew just how enthusiastically much of occupied Europe had greeted *The Moon Is Down*. Long before the war ended, the noisy American dispute over the book had abated; after the war, the political and philosophical arguments it had spawned seemed moot. Today, although references to *The Moon*

AMERICAN RECEPTION

Is Down often mention its warm reception in various Nazi-occupied countries, almost nothing has been written about how the work came to be translated and distributed in those countries, about the reasons for its popularity, and finally, about how widespread and deeply rooted that popularity was.

2

Norway

N 16 JANUARY 1963, back at home in New York one month after receiving the Nobel Prize for litera-ture, Steinbeck wrote to his longtime Norwegian pub-lisher, Harald Grieg, whom Steinbeck had visited during his trip to Stockholm. After a circuitous disparagement of his recent honor ("I have never been one for medals or decorations. They seem a kind of vanity that doesn't touch me"), Steinbeck recalled an award that had meant very much to him: the Haakon VII Cross, bestowed personally by the king in Oslo in 1946. Three or four years after that presentation, Steinbeck's older son, then six, had become fond of the cross, had worn it (with his father's permission) to school, and had lost it. For twelve years or so Steinbeck had been shy about mentioning the matter to his Norwegian friends, but now he wondered whether Grieg could get him a duplicate: "I would be very pleased to have it. It was a reminder of the old hard true days when men were better and braver than they

could be. I believe I remember that when I got it, Norway was so poor that I had to pay for the cross, I mean the cost of it. And I would be awfully glad to do that again."[1]

So it was that John Steinbeck, even during the heady rush of resurgent fame only weeks after he had been awarded the most coveted of all literary prizes, was preoccupied with thoughts of another medal given him in Scandinavia sixteen years earlier—one virtually unknown outside that part of the world. He had been chosen to receive the Haakon VII Cross because he had written *The Moon Is Down*. In the judgment of the king of Norway himself, that novel had bolstered the morale of his entire war-ravaged nation.

Steinbeck's reputation was solidly established in Norway even before the German invasion. Harald Grieg's firm, Gyldendal Norsk Forlag (Gyldendal Norwegian Publishers), had issued translations of *Tortilla Flat* in 1938, *Of Mice and Men* in 1939, and *The Grapes of Wrath* in 1940.[2] No translations of Steinbeck were published in Norway from the middle of 1940 until the middle of 1945, the period of German occupation, but by late 1942 the Norwegian-language edition of a fourth Steinbeck title—this one printed in Sweden—was being clandestinely distributed throughout Norway by Nazi-banned organizations.

This novel, *The Moon Is Down*, would achieve popularity in several Nazi-occupied countries, but it came to have singular significance for Norwegians because they believed it was about Norway—a perception shared, incidentally, by other Europeans. Actually, *The Moon Is Down* is set in an unnamed country, although details of the plot and setting do indeed suggest Norway. The manner of the fictional invasion (sudden and without correct diplomatic preliminaries) as well as the narrator's observation that during January it is dark by three o'clock in the afternoon and not light again until nine in the morning would in 1942 have implied either Norway or Denmark, both overrun by surprise attacks on 9 April 1940. But the immediate harshness of the occupation that followed, the rapid development of a popular resistance movement, the presence of a local quisling, and avalanches in nearby mountains would all have evoked Norway.

The idea that *The Moon Is Down* portrays the Nazi invasion of Norway persists in Europe. Everyone this writer interviewed there nearly forty years after the clandestine editions were circulated was sure of Steinbeck's intent. European certainty about the matter is also apparent in the specific reference to setting given in the 1943 British edition of the play version. "The action of the play occurs in a small mining town in Norway. The time is 1941."[3] The American edition of the play, published in 1942, makes no reference either to Norway or to a specific time. During the war Steinbeck himself encouraged the notion that he had intended a Norwegian setting, perhaps because Norwegians were so appreciative of what they perceived as sympathy for their plight. In the forlagets efterskrift (publisher's postscript) to a 1943 edition of *Maanen er gaaet ned*, one of the clandestine Danish translations of *The Moon Is Down*, Steinbeck says, "My book *The Moon Is Down* is built entirely upon the Norwegian people's unconquerable will to achieve victory."[4] In a conversation with Budd Schulberg, he alludes to the Norwegians standing up to the Nazis in *The Moon Is Down*.[5] Steinbeck does, however, explain in his 1963 article "Reflections on a Lunar Eclipse" that he had placed his novel in no particular country.[6]

Sometime before December 1942 a copy of *The Moon Is Down*, first published in the United States in March of that year, made its way to Stockholm. There it came to the attention of the Press Division of the loyalist Norwegian Legation, whose members were responsible for smuggling into Norway books, periodicals, and newspapers from the United States, England, and Sweden.[7] The legation instructed a forty-year-old fellow exile named Nils Lie (died 1978), then chief consultant of Gyldendal, to translate the novel for illegal distribution in his homeland. Lie was preparing to leave Sweden for London, where he would spend the remaining war years editing a Norwegian magazine and scouting out books for peacetime publication by Gyldendal, but he stayed in Stockholm long enough to complete the translation and to deliver it to Åhlén and Åkerlunds, a publishing firm with which he had worked closely before the occupation.[8]

Nils Lie in the mid-1960s.
(Courtesy of Gyldendal Norsk Forlag)

That the Norwegians in Sweden had *The Moon Is Down* translated before smuggling it into Norway attests to their confidence in its power to boost morale there. The time, labor, and expense involved precluded translation of all but a few carefully selected books; thus most reading matter arriving at the legation was simply sent along as received, in English or Swedish.[9] According to Oslo journalist and writer Arne Skouen, however, there was no doubt that *The Moon Is Down* deserved special treatment. Its translation "was a matter of course ... considering John Steinbeck's high standing in Scandinavian literature and the content of the novel, which had an immense appeal to people in occupied countries." Skouen also recalls that Nils Lie himself had regarded the novel as "a natural" for Norway.[10]

Printing the Norwegian-language edition of *The Moon Is Down* posed no difficulties in Sweden, diplomatic or otherwise. Their official neutrality notwithstanding, Swedes were clearly sympathetic to Norwegians. Contracts for books destined for underground distribution in Norway were therefore commonplace in Stockholm by 1942,[11] although according to John Dahl, assistant librarian in the Norwegian Department of the Oslo University Library, most clandestine publications circulated in Norway during the war were printed inside Norway.[12] Since Åhlén and Åkerlunds no longer have records for that year, it is uncertain exactly how many copies of Lie's translation were published or in what month, but Gordon Hølmebakk, current editor-in-chief of Gyldendal, remembers a Swedish friend's once mentioning that the edition ran to several thousand.[13] The Norwegian-language edition itself was a small, unpretentious volume whose physical appearance betrayed its intended use: Measuring about 7½ by 4½ inches and printed on tissue-thin paper, it wore a soft paper cover, the usual clothing of clandestine books. On the cover its Norwegian title was stamped in bold block letters: *Natt uten måne* (literally, *Night without Moon*).

The first illegal shipment of *Natt uten måne* was delivered, probably sometime in the fall of 1942, to Norwegians hungry for uncensored news and literature, an appetite whetted by the "cultural cleansing" of their publishers, bookstores, and libraries begun in the first months of occupation. Nils Lie's superior at Gyldendal, Chief Editor Harald Grieg, had been imprisoned. In his place the Nazis had installed the son of Norwegian collaborationist author Knut Hamsun. The elder Hamsun (originally Knut Pedersen) was a novelist and playwright who had won the Nobel Prize in 1920 and who, according to historian William Ebenstein, was the only author of world reputation to praise Nazism publicly.[14] Books by writers hostile to the Nazis or otherwise undesirable had been removed from the shelves of Oslo's public library. Retired Gyldendal employee Frits von

2918 *A*

Mappe **39.**
Ekspl. **11 7/12**
Årg.
o v. **1 / /**

NATT
UTEN
MÅNE

Front cover of one of the copies of the clandestine Norwegian translation of *The Moon Is Down* confiscated south of Oslo at Ski on 11 December 1942, as indicated by the imprint of the Norwegian Nazi police, top right. *(Courtesy of the University of Oslo and Gyldendal Norsk Forlag)* der Lippe says that just after Norway's liberation in May 1945, officials at the library found three thousand such books which had been hidden away earlier by the Nazis.[15] Among them were works of Steinbeck, Einstein, Freud, Gide, Gorki, Heine, Dreiser, Hemingway, and Sinclair Lewis.

Censorship, in fact, reached into every hamlet in Norway, but so did the publications sent in by the Norwegian Legation in Stockholm. The route such contraband traveled from Stockholm to Norway depended on its nature. Highly confidential documents (those, for example, that might compromise the patriotic underground) were hand-carried across the thousand-mile border between Sweden and Norway at points where the German guard was ineffective. Less sensitive material, such as *Natt uten måne*, usually came by regular rail lines. Svein Johs Ottesen, at the time of his interview an editor of Oslo's *Aftenposten*, remembers being told that copies were dropped from airplanes along with a volume of poetry written by Norwegian patriot Nordahl Grieg, the brother of Gyldendal chief editor Harald Grieg.[16] But this method of distribution, according to John Dahl, was so expensive that it was rarely used. The train from Stockholm to Oslo, on the other hand, was used frequently. Oddvar Aas, then a member of the Norwegian Legation in Sweden, says that by 1942 hardly a train on that route arrived without a cache of proscribed cargo, most of which got through because of the volume of baggage and commercial crates surrounding it. The Nazis simply could not examine everything. Of course they did intercept illegal shipments occasionally.

One episode of confiscation led to an official report which not only revealed the precise date when *Natt uten måne* was first discovered in Norway by the Quisling government but also underscored the unusual significance attached to the book by the Nazi leadership in Norway. Kjell Larsgaard, who has collected material for a bibliography of clandestine World War II newspapers in Norway, found a copy of that report among surviving records of the Statspolitiet—the Nazified Norwegian police.

> [On] December 11, 1942, the Police for Price and Rationing confiscated some luggage on the train leaving Ski (29 km. south of Oslo) for Oslo at 21:28. The train was coming on the so-called Eastern line. At the control [station] no one would claim ownership [of] the luggage, because it was courier-baggage from Sweden. The contents were: some food and articles of luxury, compasses, covers for maps, some pistol ammunition and accessories, 401 pamphlets, press cuttings and books. The printed matter was chiefly published or issued by Norwegian and Allied authorities. Among the books confiscated were 36 copies of Steinbeck's *Natt uten måne*. Some copies of these

illegal prints were handed over to the Security Police (Norwegian and German) and to the nazified Press Directorate. [On] December 18, 1942, 6 copies of the confiscated books were brought to the Head of the Staff of Adjutants, to "Ministerpresident" Quisling, and to Captain Langlie at the Royal Palace in Oslo by the State Police for the Oslo and Aker District. The accompanying note ran: "The enclosed 6 items were together with other objects confiscated in a train control [station] some days ago. It is the first time the police have come across a Norwegian translation of John Steinbeck's famous book *The Moon Is Down*." The note is signed by K. A. Marthinsen, Head of the State Police, Major General.[17]

The man Marthinsen refers to as "Ministerpresident" Quisling was none other than the Norwegian fascist Vidkun Quisling, whose name added to the English language a new word for traitor. Leader of the Nazi-inspired Norwegian National Unity Party, or *Nasjonal Samling*, Quisling had begun conspiring with the Germans as early as 1939, when he journeyed to Berlin to encourage various Nazi leaders—including Hitler himself—to invade his homeland. Hitler was so obsessed with secrecy that he kept even his Norwegian admirer in the dark about invasion plans before the attack on 9 April. Undiscouraged by the Führer's slight, Quisling proclaimed himself prime minister of Norway

Vidkun Quisling, leader of the Nazi-inspired Norwegian National Unity Party and minister president of Norway during the German occupation. His name became a synonym for traitor. (*Courtesy of Gyldendal Norsk Forlag*)

less than twenty-four hours after the German landing. When he tried to enlist the support of Norwegian businessmen, labor leaders, public officials, army officers, and intellectuals, however, they rebuffed him. The self-proclaimed leader was so scorned throughout Norway, in fact, that Hitler had to withdraw his support, and Quisling was forced out of office after only six days. Not quite two years later having somehow increased the membership in his *Nasjonal Samling* party to forty thousand, Quisling was back in favor with Berlin. In January 1942 the Germans offered him the post of minister president, which he assumed on 1 February 1942, nearly a year before Major-General Marthinsen delivered to him the confiscated copies of *Natt uten måne*.[18]

Quite apart from what *Natt uten måne* may have contributed to anti-Nazi feeling among the Norwegian people (and the Marthinsen memo provides testimony that it was fueling enough resentment to worry the highest echelon), Quisling, who never gained public support, had a personal reason for concern. The only wholly contemptible character in the novel, the only character disdained by the townspeople and their quasi-Nazi invaders alike, is the Quisling-like fifth columnist, Mr. Corell, whose name in Steinbeck's galley proofs was a pejorative portmanteau: Curseling.[19] Late in the novel, an attempt by the popular resistance to murder Corell was a point of explicit significance not likely to be overlooked by either the minister president or the resentful people he nominally governed. In the course of events, Quisling managed to survive until the liberation—when he was arrested, tried for treason, found guilty, and executed. Major General Marthinsen, on the other hand, was liquidated by the resistance a few months before the end of the war. In retaliation, the Nazis shot thirty-four Norwegians.[20]

Once illegal shipments of *Natt uten måne* made their way past control stations, the Norwegian resistance, crafty and effective after two and one-half years of circumventing German officials, took the books to reliable compatriots, who were asked to pass them around among trustworthy friends. Frits von der Lippe, chief secretary at Gyldendal from 1930 to 1949, tells how he became such a local distributor.

> An astonishing thing happened in 1943. In the middle of the day in Oslo's main thoroughfare, Karl Johan Street, among uniformed people and civilians who might be dangerous, a man came up on the side of me and said, whispering, "Follow me. I have something for you. Something you shall distribute." I knew the face, but not the name. I said to him, "Why here, now?" He said, "I came this morning, and I leave tonight, when I have delivered what I have in the suitcase." "Back to Sweden?" I said. "Yes." Then we

went from Karl Johan over to Stortengade, the next street, and went into a house with an elevator with seven stops and traveled up and down, up and down, until we were alone. Then this man gave me four or five packages and said, "Go straight home." And he put me out on the fifth stop and went down the elevator, and I've not seen him since. I went home and opened up one of the small packages and found the small copies of *Natt uten måne*.[21]

Norwegians who got the little books from intermediaries like von der Lippe circulated them so extensively that of perhaps thousands of copies brought into Norway, few survive today; most were completely tattered by constant use.

The popular acceptance of *The Moon Is Down* in occupied Norway became clear soon after the war. Norway was liberated on 8 May 1945. Nils Lie returned immediately to Gyldendal, where a decision was made to bring out forthwith a new edition of Steinbeck's book. Lie reviewed the translation he had done three years earlier in Stockholm, and then von der Lippe made a few corrections before dispatching it to the printers. Except for these corrections, the text is that of the clandestine version. Around the middle of June, the new edition was in Norwegian bookstores. Two printings of ten thousand copies each quickly sold out, at a time when an average printing for a novel in Norway consisted of one or two thousand copies.[21] Complementing the extraordinary postwar commercial success of the novel, the play version of *The Moon Is Down* was performed in Oslo's National Theater when the season opened in September.

On 14 November 1946 Steinbeck flew to Oslo for the official presentation of the Haakon VII Cross, the personal medal of the popular wartime king, a medal given only to those who had distinguished themselves by outstanding service to Norway during the war. Steinbeck's visit, although much anticipated by an admiring public, had an inauspicious beginning. Scarcely had he settled in his hotel room when he was hurried away to meet the Norwegian press corps. Always discomposed by press publicity, he braced himself (and alarmed his hosts) by tossing off several glasses of schnapps. Frits von der Lippe recalls that first night of Steinbeck's visit.

> Because I was chief secretary at Gyldendal at the time, I went up to Fornebu [airport just outside Oslo] and charmed Mr. Steinbeck and his friend Bo Beskow, who has painted him, and then took them to the Grand Hotel. It was cold and raining and snowing, and Steinbeck was tired out. So I said, "You are cold, Mr. Steinbeck? You want something to warm you up?" "Yes," he said. "A cup of tea?" I asked in my naïveté. And he stared at me, the first Norwegian he met, and he thought he had arrived in an absolutely mad country. "So, what else?" I asked him. "A

schnapps," he said. And then I went down to the restaurant and met a man I knew there, and I said, "Go down to the hotel center and find the best Norwegian schnapps you have in the house and bring it up immediately." And he came up with a whole bottle. Mr. Beskow got so much, and I got so much, and so much was left. And the rest—Mr. Steinbeck was drinking it in big glasses. The whole bottle! I was afraid. I couldn't stop it, but I worried about the press conference. We had invited all the Norwegian papers. I don't remember how many, but it was a lot of people. They were sitting down there waiting for him, and so I said, "We must go, Mr. Steinbeck." "One glass more," he said. But you couldn't see it on him. He was quite all right. And then the Norwegian author and journalist Arne Skouen came in; he was to lead the press conference.

We went down, and the conference was at first rather in doubt. Silly questions. A man from *Aftenposten,* our biggest paper in Norway, asked Steinbeck if he wrote his novels with a pen or with a typewriter. Mr. Beskow took me by the arm—so hard that I had blue marks the next day—and said, "One more schnapps for Mr. Steinbeck!" So I ran to the kitchen and was seeking, as if somebody was dying, a double schnapps for a world-famous author. I got it and ran back. I couldn't get next to Mr. Steinbeck but was sitting quite near him. "Please," I said to Beskow, "what should I do with it?" "Take it to him! Take it to him!" I did, and he swallowed it. And then the press conference went off quite nicely.

Steinbeck and Bo Beskow *(left)* at Beskow's farm near Löderup in southern Sweden, June 1957. *(Courtesy of Bo Beskow and Elaine Steinbeck)*

Bo Beskow, the friend von der Lippe mentions as having accompanied Steinbeck to Oslo, was a well-known Swedish painter who had become close to Steinbeck since they first met in New York in 1936. Beskow had a slightly different recollection of the press conference. When this writer talked with him in Sweden on 23 May 1981, two days after the interview with von der Lippe, he said that Steinbeck had been too exhausted to get to the conference on time. Because the waiting Norwegian press corps assumed he was playing prima donna, they were mildly indignant by the time Steinbeck arrived there. The "silly questions" were intended to embarrass Steinbeck. Beskow sent von der Lippe for another schnapps because he knew that Steinbeck—ill at ease with the press under the best of circumstances—needed additional fortification.

After the precarious press conference, the evening took a lighter turn as Steinbeck attended a dinner in his honor. Von der Lippe resumes his narrative.

> Then we went to one of the big Norwegian dinners in the home of my director, Harald Grieg. I looked at all the glasses on the table, and then I looked at Steinbeck. There was sherry for the soup, white wine for the fish, red wine for the meat, port wine for the dessert, and coffee and cognac. I couldn't see how he was going to do it. But after the coffee and cognac he stopped drinking. Then all of us got as much whiskey as we wanted, but he was drinking only soda water. I don't know how it is in America, but it's customary in Norway for the man honored at a dinner to make a little speech to thank the hostess. Someone whispered to Steinbeck that he should do that. And he rose and said, "I never worried about such a speech, and I can't make such a speech, but I can sing a little song." And then he sang in honor of Mrs. Grieg, sitting beside her, and it was a bit naughty.

Von der Lippe has forgotten the song, but Bo Beskow remembered it and sang it for me.

> Oh, the captain thought that Kitty
> Was so very, very pretty
> That he hit her on the titty
> With a soft boiled egg.

Beskow's tempo got slower and slower as he pronounced the five words of the last line, his voice dropping one note on each word and fading away in a droll basso profundo.

Von der Lippe concludes his account with events of the next day. "I went down to the Grand Hotel and brought Steinbeck up to the Royal Palace. After that I did not see him again, but I am told he had a very nice, cozy chat with the king." In the royal palace King Haakon VII presented the medal to Steinbeck for his contribution, through *The Moon Is Down*, to Norway's freedom. It was the very medal, lost by his son at school, that Steinbeck was so eager to replace over a decade and a half later—a medal that must have reminded him how gratefully his novel had been received in a nation dispirited by defeat and occupation.

A large measure of their enthusiastic response to *The Moon Is Down* may be attributed to Norwegians' conviction that the novel depicts the German occupation of their land. Von der Lippe remembers Steinbeck's saying during the press conference that he intended a Norwegian setting in *The Moon Is Down,* "especially because the next day he was to go to our king, who would give him the war medal, which is given to Norwegians and foreigners who in some way worked for Norway—took part in the war for Norway. The king had chosen Steinbeck for *The Moon Is Down.*"

At the time *The Moon Is Down* appeared there near the end of 1942, in any event, Norway felt forgotten even by free and friendly countries, whose attention was now commanded by great battles in Russia, North Africa, and the Pacific. *The Moon Is Down* told Norwegians not only that they were remembered but that the contumacious spirit and sheer pluck of three million people defying Nazi authority was known to the world. In a newspaper review written shortly after the publication of the first postwar edition of the novel, a critic named Molaug recalls that when Norwegians had read the clandestine version during the occupation, "the words [had fallen] like manna in a hungry soul."[22] Journalist Svein Johs Ottesen believes that at least some of the appeal of *The Moon Is Down* in Norway may be attributed to his fellow citizens' feeling flattered that an American author of international fame had written a book about them. Such attention assured a sympathetic response, even though "Norwegians in general found [the novel] a bit curious, [since] it was not Norwegian in tone, setting, and names of the people."[23]

Nor was *The Moon Is Down* the only evidence Norwegians had of Steinbeck's concern for them. Three years after they were invaded, he sent them a special message, one which seems, in fact, to summarize the main theme of *The Moon Is Down*. The message appeared in the mimeographed Norwegian underground paper *Bulletinen* in May 1943.

> The American author John Steinbeck sends this greeting to Norway: "I believe that when Germany at last is defeated on the battlefield, the nation will have already lost the battle in quite a different way. When the grey troops, armed with weapons and falsehood invaded Norway, they were supposed to win this war, but it was then already lost. It was lost in the cold, hostile eyes of children and mothers. It was lost among the Norwegian soldiers who fought up to the mountains, where they buried their rifles and uniforms, and returned to the cities to fight with their brains. It was lost among the teachers and the ministers [of the churches] who refused to co-operate, although they knew the punishment."[24]

For Oddvar Aas, the explanation for the novel's popularity was obvious. It "raised discussions . . . and free discussions were highly appreciated under Nazi occupation. It was cleaning the air!"[25] Frits von der Lippe remembers that the novel fed his compatriots' "hunger for sympathy" and that Norwegians were gratified that Steinbeck was able to describe exactly how the Norwegians felt about the Nazis and about the resistance.

The perception that Steinbeck had somehow divined their deepest feelings about the occupation was probably the main reason Norwegians found *The Moon Is Down* so appealing. Those feelings, according to Molaug, were

> all there in the book: there were our problems, our hopes, our sorrows about [Germany's] victory. And we read with eagerness the sure understanding—the analysis of Steinbeck. He had a good conception; he could see so clearly their hated system. It was like a refreshing bath to read it; it made you feel so good after a day's splashing in the Nazi propaganda and deceit.

An anonymous reviewer in Arendal's *Vestlandske Tidende* for 3 July 1945 concurs.

> The novel was something we all felt, and there you found the explanation of a lot of things that inspired us to fight against those who had the power. The meaningless fight—[Steinbeck] understood that. A lot of things that are hidden within the people that are living in a small country, Steinbeck brought it all out. He had insight. And especially into [Norwegians'] reaction against the ones who took over the country.

... And in its quiet action [*The Moon Is Down*] gives
the background for this strange war that we couldn't
really read in the history book.[26]

Steinbeck's remarkable reading of the Norwegian
national mood during the occupation was what caught
the attention of William Colby, one of the very few
American observers on the scene. Colby, later director
of the Central Intelligence Agency under Presidents
Nixon and Ford, was leader of a special operations unit
of ski paratroopers attached to the OSS. Of that group of
thirty-nine enlisted men and three officers, sixteen were
dropped successfully into northern Norway on Palm
Sunday of 1945. Colby's mission was to cut vital north-
south transportation lines and thereby forestall the shifting of 500,000 German soldiers in Norway to the western front.[27] Because he had read *The Moon Is Down* just
after its American publication three years earlier, and
because his assignment brought him into contact with
Norwegians while their country was still under German
control, Colby is uniquely qualified to judge how well
Steinbeck had spoken for them. "I was tremendously
impressed by the basic theme of *The Moon Is Down*, i.e.
the degree to which ordinary Norwegian citizens ab-
stained from contact or relationships with the Germans.
This attitude was perhaps dramatized by a young lady I

met who had not been to a movie in five years because the movies were controlled by the Germans."[28]

When Norwegian writers turned to a public discussion of *The Moon Is Down* following the liberation, their appreciation for Steinbeck's ideas and for the comfort those ideas had given Norway during the most traumatic years of its national existence was undiminished by sober retrospection. The critic Moulag voiced that appreciation most memorably in his simple conclusion about the place of the novel in Norway's history. "*The Moon Is Down* is the epic of the [Norwegian] underground."

3

Denmark

 OGENS STAFFELDT'S
bookstore on the bottom
floor of Dagmar House on
Copenhagen's Town Hall
Square bustled with more activity than usual early in
1943, and not merely because Danes were stocking their
libraries during the third dismal winter under German
occupation. Staffeldt had only recently finished printing
illegal editions of several proscribed titles, among them a
Danish translation of *The Moon Is Down*, and the extra
traffic around his shop was that of innocent-looking
students from Danish patriotic groups who came on
bicycles to fetch packages of these books for delivery to
trustworthy merchants. Ironically, Dagmar House also
served as Gestapo headquarters in Copenhagen, but that
inconvenience never deterred Staffeldt's clandestine operations; in fact, on several occasions he beckoned passing Gestapo officers and asked them to help the strug-
gling students load their bundles.[1] Hefting packages for
Danes was the kind of assistance the Gestapo was still

eager to give at that time in a country Nazi officials were hoping would remain a relatively docile "model protectorate." Meanwhile the spectacle of the enemy's secret police scrambling about in unwitting service of partisans offered Staffeldt and his student associates a rare opportunity for mirth during those unhappy days.

Staffeldt's brisk business in anti-German literature, one of many patriotic enterprises cropping up all over Denmark by the end of 1942 and the beginning of 1943, was evidence that the Danish populace had had enough. After enduring for over two and one-half years the indignities of Nazi occupation, they had begun actively to oppose German authority. That change of public attitude prefigured the development of a coordinated national resistance movement. Such a movement had taken longer to evolve in Denmark than in Norway, where sabotage units had sprung to action immediately after the German military defeat of Norwegian regular forces. During the first year of occupation, in fact, only a dozen or so illegal leaflets were distributed in all of Denmark, and the first sabotage operations in Copenhagen did not occur until late 1941.[2]

There were good reasons for the belated growth of the Danish resistance. Certainly geography disfavored Denmark. A virtually flat country less than one-seventh the size of Norway, it lacks the rugged mountains and extensive forests that so effectively served Norwegian partisans as hideouts and staging areas. With German forces storming across the Danish frontier and the Luftwaffe poised to strike Danish cities, Danes had understood the futility of a sustained defense in the face of crushing German military superiority. Only hours after the German attack they had agreed to accept occupation rather than to subject Danish cities to the destruction the Nazis had threatened if the Danish government decided otherwise. In addition to its geographical disadvantages, Denmark was also politically and militarily isolated. According to Jørgen Hæstrup, even Winston Churchill had acknowledged the gravity of the situation there. Loath as he was ever to concede anything to Hitler, the British prime minister was forced to admit in a confidential meeting with war correspondents in February 1940 that nothing could be done to help Denmark if the Nazis invaded. "Denmark is so frightfully near Germany that it would be impossible to bring help. I, at all events, would not take the responsibility of guaranteeing Denmark." Essentially, Denmark faced disaster if it did not surrender.[3]

The Norwegians, enjoying a far more defensible terrain, chose to give the Germans a stiff fight. By the time German forces defeated Norwegian regulars in June 1940, Norwegians had decided to keep battling the invader through guerrilla warfare and were organized to do so. In Norway, then, resistance activities simply represented a continuation of fighting; in Denmark there was virtually no fighting to continue. The Danes were not only "stunned into indolence"[4] by the suddenness of the German attack but also lulled by the initial correctness of German behavior in Denmark. The ultimatum which Berlin delivered to Copenhagen on 9 April 1940 included a promise that Germany would respect Denmark's political integrity. Accordingly, the legal Danish government remained in power after accepting the ultimatum. For the first two and one-half years of the occupation, that government—the Danes' own—presented yet another obstacle to the growth of the Danish resistance.

In order to confront the crises of occupation with a government as representative as possible, the Social-Democratic coalition which had acquiesced to the German ultimatum of 9 April reconstituted itself later in the year as a national coalition embracing all major Danish political parties. For more than two years this government struggled to serve its people as a buffer against the Germans by mitigating the harshness of occupation through negotiations, formal protests, and dilatory parliamentary maneuvers. Danish politicians—indeed most Danes—understood the speciousness of German pledges not to interfere in Danish internal affairs, but they also believed that if the Danish government retained legal, if not entirely de facto, authority, the few concessions that might be wrung from the Germans would be preferable to the greater perils of direct Nazi rule. Thus until 29 August 1943, when the Danish government resigned rather than accede to unconscionable German demands, it strove to maintain a modus vivendi with the occupation authorities.[5]

That policy, enjoying the support of the majority of the Danish people, required the Danish government to pass strict laws against acts of resistance and any other expressions of anti-German feeling likely to disturb the delicate political counterpoise. Denmark's most fervent patriots were perforce throttled by their own government and compelled to become criminals according to the laws of their own country in order to serve it. The problem was peculiar to Denmark. The citizens of other Nazi-occupied nations of western Europe, deprived immediately of legal, popularly elected governments and thus earlier embittered by the rigors of either direct or puppet Nazi rule, always looked more favorably upon their patriotic resistance. But in Denmark, for at least the first two and one-half years of the occupation, the resistance threatened what precarious security Danes had managed to salvage from their distressing situation.

Of course not all Danes approved of their government's cautious approach to dealing with the Germans. Even at the very beginning of the occupation, an obstreperous minority had denounced the policy which, given the transpicuous evils of Nazism, they considered tainted. Thus they urged the resignation of the Danish government, a maneuver which would remove not only the offense of Danish submission to tyranny but also the troublesome domestic legal obstacles to resistance activities. These early activists realized that life would be more perilous in their country after the Germans usurped complete control of the Danish government, but they were convinced that Denmark's response to Nazi barbarism touched moral issues far too significant for Danes to be thinking primarily of personal safety.

One organization of early activists dedicated to breaking up the Danish government's modus vivendi with the Germans was De Danske Studenter (The Danish Students), an offshoot of the multifarious partisan alliance Frit Danmark (Free Denmark). From April 1942 until the end of the war, this group published the semiofficial resistance newspaper. In the autumn of 1941 a cadre of young Danes later influential in the student organization helped orchestrate the first serious outburst of anti-German sentiment in Copenhagen: a demonstration at Amalienborg (the royal palace) provoked by Hitler's coercing the Danish government to sign the Anti-Comintern Pact.[6] A year later, De Danske Studenter would seize yet another opportunity to express their dissatisfaction with the modus vivendi when they decided to publish a Danish-language edition of *The Moon Is Down*.

One of the organizers of the student demonstration at Amalienborg and, subsequently, of De Danske Studenter, was Jørgen Jacobsen, later a well-known lawyer in Copenhagen. Shortly before Christmas of 1942 a friend from the student group brought Jacobsen a copy of the American edition of *The Moon Is Down* and asked him to translate it into Danish. Jacobsen, then a twenty-three-year-old law student, remembers the episode well.

> The man who came with [the copy of the novel] was a student of medicine called Ib Zacho. I don't know if he is still alive. He was a very nervous man. I didn't know him under that name; he was under an assumed name. He was called Peter Utsen or something like that. He was one of the people I worked with. I lived at that time in Amager [peninsula just south of Copenhagen]. I had been married in April '42 and had my first house there. He came, I remember, with the book and asked me to translate it, and I accepted and did the translation with a friend of mine called Paul Lang, who was also a student of law. We did it here in Copenhagen in his flat in Roskildevej. In a week—it took us a week. We worked day and night and just translated it as best we could, with a *Concise Oxford* in one hand and a glass of beer in the other. I was very

nervous. I thought the Gestapo was at my heels. As a matter of fact, they didn't ever know of my existence.[7]

The most difficult part of the novel to translate was the title. Finding a suitable one in Danish was problematic because a literal translation would not have suggested what Tetsumaro Hayashi has referred to as a "lunar condition [which] is the equivalent of the human condition" in the novel: a dark, moonless night with its attendant implication of the evil and spiritual despair brought by the Nazis.[8] The title Jacobsen settled on, *Maanen er skjult (The Moon Is Hidden)*, carries all the appropriate connotations. After Jacobsen and Lang finished their translation, an anonymous comrade from De Danske Studenter delivered it for printing to another member of that organization, Jørgen Kieler, who worked on it in his apartment at 2 Raadhusstræde in Copenhagen.[9] A very short time later, other printers with connections to De Danske Studenter were hastily assembling clandestine editions of *Maanen er skjult*. Among them was Mogens Staffeldt of the busy bookstore in Dagmar House.

Staffeldt, then in his late twenties, had been involved in resistance activities from the day the Germans invaded his country. On 9 April 1940, annoyed that Denmark had capitulated without a fight, he had driven members of the Polish embassy to a rendevous with an English

Jørgen Jacobsen in 1942. *(Courtesy of Jørgen Jacobsen)*

submarine off the north coast of Zealand.[10] Staffeldt got married on 15 August 1942, honeymooned for several weeks, and then upon his return to Copenhagen enlisted his wife, Grete, to type material for underground distribution.

Mrs. Staffeldt began her work around the end of September in a seventeenth-century house on Overgaden Weden, where two brothers, both members of De Danske Studenter, lived with their mother. Eventually, she gave her husband copies of three works to print. Staffeldt has forgotten the title of one of them, but the other two were *Return to the Future*, a scorching attack on the Nazis' New Order in Europe by the Danish-born Norwegian author and Nobel laureate Sigrid Undset, and *Maanen er skjult*. Staffeldt remembers printing *Maanen er skjult* late in the fall of 1942, but Jørgen Jacobsen recalls clearly that he and Lang did not finish their translation until Christmastime of that year. Also, at the end of their translation Jacobsen and Lang quoted statements taken from a Danish parliamentary debate which was not held until early December 1942. A possible explanation is that *Maanen er skjult* was the last of the three works Mrs. Staffeldt typed in the old house on Overgaden Weden, since she could not have received it before late December 1942 or early January of the following year.

Because he had no safe access to a printing machine, Staffeldt sold his life insurance policy for three thousand kroner (today roughly equivalent to three thousand dollars) in order to purchase a duplicator. Soon he was cranking out clandestine books in his shop on the bottom floor of Dagmar House while the Gestapo, in their headquarters on the floors above him, busied themselves with stratagems designed to quash the Danish resistance.

Mogens Staffeldt with his mimeograph machine.
(Courtesy of Grete Staffeldt)

Within a short time Staffeldt had published fifteen thousand copies each of *The Moon Is Down* and *Return to the Future*; ten thousand of each in the first printing were followed by an additional five thousand copies of each a few months later. Although Staffeldt himself sold a few copies to trusted customers, most were distributed to other booksellers or to large businesses such as banks and shipping firms, which sold them in turn to their own customers or employees. Students on bicycles picked up orders in wrapped packages from Staffeldt's bookstore—undaunted, as we have seen earlier, by the constant movement of the Gestapo in and out of the same building, night and day.

Staffeldt's having to rely on an office duplicating machine meant, of course, that he could not reduce the print size and produce a small, easily concealed booklet. The booklets he printed were all on standard-size typing paper—over twice the size of the Norwegian clandestine edition. By single-spacing on both sides of each leaf and leaving narrow margins, Staffeldt managed to crowd the entire novel onto thirty-one sheets, which he stapled together between brown, gray, or green paper covers.[11]

The sale of one thousand copies of Kieler's initial printing of *Maanen er skjult* followed by fifteen thousand copies of Staffeldt's edition leaves little doubt that the novel fulfilled one expectation of De Danske Studenter—that it would raise money for their parent organization, Frit Danmark. Jørgen Jacobsen never doubted its potential as a best-seller. "Everyone wanted to read a novel by John Steinbeck, and when the novel was about the Nazis and occupation, you could sell a lot of them, that was for sure." Each issue of the Kieler edition sold for ten kroner (today roughly equivalent to

DENMARK

Clandestine press in Copenhagen, 1944. *(Courtesy of The Museum of Denmark's Fight for Freedom, 1940–1945)*

ten dollars), with proceeds going to Frit Danmark. Jacobsen remembers particularly well his comrades' zeal about raising funds for the organization—even he had to pay for a copy of the novel he had worked so hard to translate. He also remembers that he and fellow translator Paul Lang worried about breaking copyright law. "We were very reluctant to steal Steinbeck's book. We talked about it: Isn't that illegal to sell another man's work and take the money? And then we decided, well, what the hell. We are doing it anyway."[12]

Earning money to finance Frit Danmark was certainly important to the activist members of De Danske Studenter, but their main motive for disseminating *Maanen er skjult* was a political one. They wanted to protest their government's accommodation with the Germans—a policy they knew the government was following with good intentions, but one nevertheless reprehensible. In Jacobsen's words,

> We didn't doubt that they [the Danish government] were doing what they thought was best for their country, but we believed that the better course of action was to fight the Germans simply because we had to, because this was something so evil, so bad. There was nothing else we could do. We didn't choose that. But if we wanted to have a life worth living, we had to fight them ourselves. We could not just sit back and wait.[13]

DENMARK

Another clandestine press in Copenhagen, 1944.
(Courtesy of The Museum of Denmark's Fight for Freedom, 1940–1945)

The Moon Is Down precisely conveyed the strong objection of the early activists to the Danish government's political arrangement with the occupying force simply by depicting decent and ordinarily peaceable men and women who refuse to accept such an accommodation and who choose instead to do what Jacobsen and his friends wanted the Danes to do: fight the invader because there is no other morally acceptable option. Steinbeck's characters are so assured of the justice of their cause that they are constitutionally incapable of submission to despotic authority. Their confidence is eloquently voiced near the conclusion of the novel by Mayor Orden just before he faces a firing squad for refusing to order his villagers to cease all resistance. Orden recites from Plato's *Apology* the reply Socrates gives to those who ask whether he should not be ashamed of living a provocative life which was likely, considering the poisoned political atmosphere of his day, to bring him to an untimely end. "To him I may fairly answer, 'There you are mistaken: a man who is good for anything ought not to calculate the chance of living or dying; he ought only to consider whether he is doing right or wrong.'"[14]

Socrates' words struck Jacobsen as so crucial to a proper understanding of the theme of *The Moon Is Down* that he took special pains to translate them correctly. He dusted off his schoolboy text of Plato, found the lines that appear in *The Moon Is Down*, and copied the Danish words. No other passage in the novel would convey so succinctly to Danish readers the opposition of the student movement to their government's pragmatic arrangement with the Nazis. In quoting Plato, Steinbeck invokes one of Western civilization's highest moral authorities, not merely to justify the active resistance of the villagers, but to insist that it is the only right course of action under the circumstances. This was the same course of action Jacobsen and his comrades in De Danske Studenter desperately wanted to urge upon their fellow countrymen. Danes clearly did recognize the importance of Socrates' speech. According to Mogens Knudsen, director of Gyldendal Publishers in Copenhagen, the speech was the passage from *The Moon Is Down* most frequently quoted in underground publications.[15]

Just in case Danish readers failed to discern that Socrates' speech addressed their situation no less than that of the villagers in the novel, Jacobsen and Lang printed on the last page of their translation excerpts of statements made soon after the occupation by the leaders of the Danish political parties represented in the pragmatic-minded national coalition government. All of these statements, quoted below in English translations provided by Jacobsen, discourage resistance and urge Danes to obey all laws.

The Liberal party: The government has the task of fighting all forms of provocation and sabotage and everything which is turned against the occupation force. We'll support [the government's position], for [provocation and sabotage] is of no interest for anybody. It only hurts the individual, and so the whole society. At this time it is so, that every individual, through his conduct, and through what he says, can make foreign policy. We disapprove highly of this private foreign policy.

The Conservative party: The [Prime] Minister [Erik] Scavenius has been elected with the approval of the collaborating parties and also with [that of] the Conservative party. We are representing the government, and it is clear that the government can be certain about the loyalty of the party and the support for carrying through the program under which the government gathers. With satisfaction, we have heard the prime minister say that the government would be obligated towards Parliament and would continue [the] line for cooperation that has been followed up to this moment, and which tends to strengthen the possibilities of our people, and which reaffirms that we can continue as a free people independently.

The Radical party: When the government now comes before Parliament in a new form and under another name, it meets with its own face—its own possibilities, its own will—and it is also an expression for the agreement which has been enforced on the political line, which is imminent and must be followed on account of the [overwhelming] difficulties of time and the evaluation of what the interests of our people should imply. It is the [hope] of my party that the government must be successful in gathering the whole population, and we will support every step in this direction to the best of our ability.

The Social Democratic party: We give our government our support after the declaration that has been made, and we will distance ourselves from the people who try to disturb the order and excite to sabotage.[16]

Not even politically naive Danes, if any still existed by late 1942, could have failed to see the discrepancy between the cautious submission to occupation advocated in the statements of the highest officials of the Danish government and the defiance of Mayor Orden and his people in *The Moon Is Down.* Nor could many Danes have failed to grasp the pungent implications of the discrepancy: that their political leaders, unlike Mayor Orden and Socrates, had chosen safety over principle, that the choice was wrong, and that the government's policy of accommodation must be changed if Danes were to live decently and maintain their self-respect.

The Danish-language edition of *The Moon Is Down* seems to have served its political purposes well—so well, in Jørgen Jacobsen's view, that the novel was more important to Denmark during the war than to any other country. By 1943 those pressing for a breach between the Danish government and the Germans sensed imminent success as the Danish public, chafing under an increasingly nettlesome Nazi authority, grew more supportive of open defiance. Incidents of sabotage rose from 14 in January of that year to 70 in April and then 198 in August. On 29 August the activists finally got their wish as the Danish government simply ceased functioning rather than enact draconian legislation demanded by the Germans, including the death penalty for sabotage, a ban on strikes and meetings, and direct German censorship. That night the Germans declared a military emergency and took over the government. Now with the Danish resistance facing only one adversary—the occupying power—the movement burgeoned, largely because the average Danish citizen was no longer torn between a will to resist Nazis and loyalty to a legal government devoted to maintaining at least a modicum of safety and security for its constituents by suppressing anti-German activities.[17] Before the war ended, the resistance had achieved such deadly effectiveness that the Allies declared Denmark a full fighting partner. In the words of Field Marshal Viscount Montgomery, the Danish resistance became "second to none."[18]

As Danes feared, however, the tenor of the occupa-

----farlige for Europas Nyordning.
ooOoo
Oberst Lanser sagde:"Kaptajn Loft. Der maa være Spor i Sneen.
Jeg ønsker hvert Hus undersøgt for Vaaben. Jeg ønsker hver Mand, som
er i Besiddelse af et, arresteret som Gidsel.De," sagde han til Borg-
mesteren."De bliver anbragt i Beskyttelsesarrest. Og forstaa dette.
Vi vil skyde fem, ti, hundrede for een."

Illustration inside the title page of a Danish translation of *The Moon Is Down*. The caption, titled "Threats to Europe's New Order," quotes lines near the end of chapter 4. "Colonel Lanser said, 'Captain Loft. There must be footprints in the snow. I want every house searched for weapons. I want every man who has one in his possession arrested as a hostage. You,' he said to the mayor, 'are going to be detained. And understand this, we will shoot five, ten, hundreds, for one.'" *(From the author's private collection)*

tion in their homeland changed overnight after their government abandoned power on 29 August. The Nazis gave up any remaining pretense of peaceful cooperation with the Danes and promulgated the severe new laws they had promised. The Danes responded by becoming even more openly feisty and fractious than they had been before and by giving for the first time nationwide acceptance and active support to their resistance organizations. So visible now was the Danes' hostility toward the German occupation forces and so effective their aid to the resistance that the Germans began to treat them as harshly as they had been treating the Norwegians for three and one-half years. That turn for the worse in the daily lives of Danes guaranteed that *The Moon Is Down* would continue to be widely read in Denmark. Having made its contribution to the political cause for which Jacobsen and his student organization had originally translated and published it, the novel would now be appreciated by Danish readers for its sympathetic portrayal of peaceable people beset by brutality.

The best evidence of the enduring appeal of *The Moon Is Down* in Denmark after August 1943 is that new clandestine editions continued to appear between then and October 1944, when the last of the dated volumes was printed. Some of the new editions were of yet another Danish translation: *Maanen er gaaet ned* (*The Moon Has Gone Down*), published by the Frit

Nordisk Forlag (Free Nordic Press). In a publisher's afterword the new translation included a statement about the importance of the Norwegian resistance, a statement issued by Steinbeck in commemoration of the third anniversary of the invasions of Norway and Denmark. Editions of *Maanen er gaaet ned,* like the various editions of *Maanen er skjult,* were typed and reproduced on duplicating machines, but the former had machine-printed title pages rather than the typed and hand-illustrated ones of the earlier translation.

Because the many printings in occupied Denmark of the two translations of *The Moon Is Down* were always samizdat operations, we will surely never know how many copies—or even editions—circulated throughout the country. *Besættelsestidens illegale blade og bøger* (*Illegal Pamphlets and Books of the Period of Occupation*) and its two supplements, however, provide a rough idea. At least sixteen separate editions of *Maanen er skjult* appeared: three had a publication date of 1943, and six had no date. *Maanen er gaaet ned* came out in three editions, all apparently printed in 1944.[19] The above sources, of course, list only copies accumulated in museums and libraries. Doubtless some typed editions prepared on private duplicating machines were eventually destroyed during the occupation or discarded after the liberation. Clearly, many thousands of copies of the two translations passed from hand to hand throughout occupied Denmark. Surviving copies are usually worn from heavy use.

As in Norway, the popularity of *The Moon Is Down* in Denmark did not subside when German forces finally evacuated. Gyldendal, Steinbeck's Danish publisher, decided that the novel would be an appropriate one with which to resume regular publication of his works in free Denmark. Gyldendal had published Danish translations of four Steinbeck novels before the occupation: *Tortilla Flat* in 1938, *Of Mice and Men* and *The Grapes of Wrath* in 1939, and *In Dubious Battle* in 1940. Some reprints of these titles were published even during the occupation. According to Mogens Knudsen, German censorship virtually forbade translation of British and American books. Danish publishing houses could, however, issue new printings of earlier editions of such works if it was done diplomatically. The director of Gyldendal during the occupation, a woman of considerable tact, developed the practice of translating an "innocent" German novel to show that she was not turning her back on the Third Reich and then publishing a British or American novel. Obviously, even such a tacit quid pro quo would not have excused the publication of a novel like *The Moon Is Down*.

Before issuing its postwar edition of *The Moon Is Down*, Gyldendal's director asked Mogens Knudsen, then a reader and translator for the firm, to examine the

MAANEN ER GAAET NED

ROMAN AF
John Steinbeck

Fra en Skydebane i Norge hvor de tyske Rekrutter skyder til Maals efter
9 hængte Patrioter hvoraf 2 Kvinder. I Baggrunden fjerner 2 tyske
Soldater Liget af den ene der er skudt ned.

FRIT NORDISK FORLAG
MCMXLIII

Title page of another edition of the second Danish translation of *The Moon Is Down*. The caption below the photograph reads, "From a target range in Norway, where the German recruits are using for target practice nine hanging patriots, two of whom are women. In the background two German soldiers are removing the body of one that has been shot down." *(Courtesy of The Museum of Denmark's Fight for Freedom, 1940–1945)* translation Jacobsen and Lang had done for the clandestine edition and then determine whether to rework that version or to produce a totally new one. Knudsen's verdict was that although the language of the earlier translation was often too "unsubtle" for a regular trade edition because it failed to capture the correct nuances, it would serve quite well as a model. So, using *Maanen er skjult*, and even retaining that title, Knudsen prepared a revised Danish translation which Gyldendal published in 1946 in an edition of five thousand copies. A second printing of eight thousand copies came out in 1961, and a third of ten thousand in 1962.[20] Three more followed in 1974, 1976, and 1980. Since the war, in fact, Gyldendal, of which Mogens Knudsen eventually became director, has published editions of virtually all of Steinbeck's works, including a special ten-volume collection in 1967. Several have been through multiple printings.

Mogens Staffeldt survived the war to sell—now legally—the Steinbeck titles which Gyldendal was publishing. His survival was a matter of some luck, however. On 17 February 1944 the Gestapo arrested him for sabotage—a far more dangerous enterprise than printing and distributing illegal books. Staffeldt was indeed deeply involved in such activity and was also transporting Danish Jews to safety after the order was given on 1 October 1943 to round them up for deportation to concentration camps. In the same bookstore where he had printed *Maanen er skjult*, Staffeldt had received Danish saboteurs who had parachuted back into their country after being trained in England, and he had hidden hundreds of Jews before arranging their escapes to Sweden. By the time of Staffeldt's arrest, saboteurs had become so disruptive in Denmark that the German occupation authorities were no longer interested in such "small potatoes" as printers and distributers of clandestine books. Thus Staffeldt found it convenient to confess to his lesser offenses, hoping to throw the Gestapo off the trail of his more serious ones. He told them everything about his publishing *Maanen er skjult* and about his helping Danish Jews escape.

Despite several weeks of intense interrogation, Staffeldt revealed nothing which might compromise his fellow saboteurs. Eventually he was sent to Horserød concentration camp, where he was sentenced to death. He managed to escape and make his way back to Copenhagen. There he hid with friends until the middle of November 1944, when he and fourteen other saboteurs were taken to the harbor, covered by crates of herring and three feet of ice in the cargo hold of an old fishing boat, and spirited away to safety in Sweden.[21] After the war, Mogens Staffeldt returned to his bookstore and ran it until his death in 1986. Throughout those years, John Steinbeck remained one of his best-selling authors.

4

Holland

NE OF THE provisions of the New Order imposed by the Germans after they overran the Netherlands between 10 May and 14 May 1940 required that Dutch actors who wished to continue performing in public join the Kulturkammer, a Nazi guild which held the power of censorship over all cultural life. Among those who refused to become associated with the German organization and thus found themselves unemployed was Ferdinand Sterneberg, then forty-three years old. Sometime before mid-1944 an actor friend with ties to De Bizige Bij (The Busy Bee), a patriotic clandestine publishing firm, brought Sterneberg a copy of *The Moon Is Down* and asked him to translate it. Sterneberg had translated English, French, and German plays and had already read and admired this Steinbeck work, so he quickly agreed. Using what he vaguely recalls was an English-language edition (it may have been smuggled into Holland from Norway), Sterneberg finished his task within a few weeks. "I never spent a

long time in translations. I'm too impatient for that. I must go on with it. I like [my translations] to read fluently, to keep the [same] rhythm, the melody, and all that. That's important for any work, isn't it? Do it at once and keep that sense of unity."[1]

For the Dutch title, Sterneberg chose *De vliegen-vanger* (*The Flypaper*), an allusion to a scene in chapter 5, about halfway through the novel. At this point the fictional conquered populace has developed effective means of resistance. The native coal miners have become deliberately clumsy and slow, mechanics take a long time to repair broken machinery, railway workers create accidents, and restaurant cooks oversalt and overpepper the food they serve to the invaders. The men of the conquering army who seek companionship with local women are occasionally found murdered. Most debilitating to the morale of the enemy soldiers, however, is the sullen silence, the cold obedience of the people. Excluded from normal social contacts except with each other, far from family and friends, and constantly fearful of the revenge of those they are supposed to control, the soldiers begin to crack under the strain. Near the end of chapter 5, Lieutenant Tonder, in the presence of several of his comrades, turns hysterical as he realizes that he and his fellow soldiers are trapped in hostile territory and, ironically, are really more the conquered than the conquerers.

Tonder got out his handkerchief and blew his nose, and he spoke a little like a man out of his head. He laughed embarrassedly. He said, "I had a funny dream. . . . I dreamed the Leader was crazy. . . ."

And Tonder went on laughing. "Conquest after conquest, deeper and deeper into molasses." His laughter choked him and he coughed into his handkerchief. "Maybe the Leader is crazy. Flies conquer the flypaper. Flies capture two hundred miles of new flypaper!"[2]

In the last scene of the novel, Doc Winter tells Colonel Lanser that Tonder's words, overheard by one of the local citizens, have become a patriotic rallying cry. "One of your men got out of hand one night and he said the flies had conquered the flypaper, and now the whole nation knows his words. They have made a song of it. The flies have conquered the flypaper."[3] Sterneberg recalls having had the impression that at this point in the novel "even Steinbeck pities these Germans, because they feel so unhappy in these surroundings." He also remembers deciding not to use a literal Dutch translation of the title *The Moon Is Down* because he believed it was not right for Holland.

Steinbeck drew his title from the beginning of act 2 of *Macbeth*. Just before Macbeth, on his way to murder Duncan, encounters Banquo and Fleance, Banquo asks, "How goes the night, boy?" and his son answers, "The moon is down; I have not heard the clock." The implication is that evil is about to descend on the kingdom. Although Sterneberg believed that the suggestion of spiritual darkness conveyed in the original title was appropriate for other occupied countries such as Norway and France, it was not for Holland.

> [The English and French titles] *The Moon Is Down* and also *Nuits noires* were not so good because these nights [of German occupation] for the [Dutch] people were not *noire*, were not black.... [The Dutch Resistance] did things in the night. Of course, they chose dark nights, and not when there was a full moon or many stars: but for their mind these nights were the best nights they ever lived, and they didn't feel it as a black night; no, it was a clear night.

After he completed his translation, Sterneberg delivered it to the man who had solicited it through Sterneberg's actor friend: Geert Lübberhuizen, founder of De Bizige Bij. Lübberhuizen's edition of *De vliegenvanger*, printed by Fokke Tamminga in The Hague, was unusually professional for an illegal underground imprint. Measuring about 7 ½ by 11 inches and covered with heavy white paper, the 124-page translation came complete with colophon. The edition was set in Egmont type, a detail noted in the colophon perhaps with irony, since the name Egmont would have evoked for Dutch patriots memories of the great Flemish freedom fighter Count Egmont (1522-68), who was executed by the duke of Alba for leading a movement to resist King Phillip II's suppression of the Netherlands' bid for independence from Spain. Printed on special old Dutch paper, *De vliegenvanger* was published in an edition of 1,025 copies, of which 25 were numbered separately and contained water-colored illustrations prepared by hand. Sterneberg is identified on the title page as the translator only by his nom de guerre, Tjebbo Hemelrijk. (Hemelrijk, meaning "sky" or "heaven," is a pun on his real name, which means "star mountain"; Tjebbo was taken from the surname Tjebbels, which Sterneberg had used earlier during the occupation on falsified identity papers.) The several illustrations in *De vliegenvanger* are attributed to Michael Gurney, the pseudonym of Sariochim Salim.

De Bizige Bij normally gave the proceeds from the sales of its clandestine publications to a general fund for the Dutch resistance. The money collected from the sales of *De vliegenvanger*, however, was all directed to a relief fund for those actors who had refused to join the Nazi-sponsored Kulturkammer.[4] Sterneberg remembers that the copies he sold were priced at one hundred guilders apiece, today roughly equivalent to a sum between two and three hundred dollars. The total earnings from the thousand-odd copies of *De vliegenvanger*, then, provided more than token aid for unemployed actors.

Unaware that Steinbeck had written a play version of *The Moon Is Down*, Sterneberg improvised one from his translation of the novel—a task he found not difficult for the curious reason that "there is not much dialogue in it." In any event, he later had reason for pride in his dramatization: after the war when he discovered Steinbeck's play version, he found it "almost the same" as his own. Soon after rendering *The Moon Is Down* into his native language, Sterneberg was giving dramatic readings from *De vliegenvanger* to patriotic Dutch audiences. "I started in '44 after I translated it and made my version of it as a play. And then I did it . . . not only in Amsterdam, but, well, in the country and in The Hague." Immediately before and just after these engagements, Sterneberg and his friends sold copies of his high-priced translations of the novel.

Sterneberg usually presented his one-man show to audiences of between twenty-five and fifty people, whom he always prepared for the possibility of a raid. "I told my audience before I started that if there were difficulties, they [were to pretend that they] were here for a lecture about a theater, and that I had [the text of such a lecture] here, and the moment [the police] enter I [will] go over to another subject, so don't look astonished, because that would spoil the whole thing."

Illustrations opposite the title page of the Dutch translation. In twenty-five special copies, such illustrations were water-colored by hand. *(Courtesy of Ferdinand Sterneberg)*

In all, Sterneberg gave more than fifty performances of *De vliegenvanger* without ever being disturbed by the Nazi authorities. He would have given more, but a personal obligation severely restricted the amount of time he could spend away from his apartment.

> I was hiding a Jewish friend and his sister . . . so I couldn't go away very long—only for a few hours or one day at the most—because they lived in a very difficult situation. In the same house [in the apartment], underneath, were . . . people who were not to be trusted. . . . I was supposed to live there by myself, so when I left the house, [my friends] couldn't talk, they couldn't leave the water running, or fill up the stove with coal, and well, I had always to be back at a certain time to see if they needed water, if they needed to refill the stove. . . . So it was very difficult for me to get away, but I did, at night and in the afternoon for some hours, and then I gave my performances. Sometimes I would go out of town and I would [take] them some other place, or someone came to replace me. It was all very difficult. [But] I succeeded in bringing them through the war.

By the autumn of 1944 Sterneberg was forced to curtail altogether his dramatic presentations of *De vliegenvanger*. In addition to the inconvenience and danger his absences caused his Jewish friends, the deprivations of war presented new obstacles.

HOLLAND

There was no railway anymore. There was a strike
that [had] started already in the autumn of '44 when
the Allies came into the south of our country.... We
all hoped in October that it was to be the end of the
war, but it wasn't. It went on until May. That was the
hardest winter we had, because there was no food
anymore, and there was no heating . . . there was no
light, there was nothing. It was a terrible winter.

Thus Sterneberg went to a great deal of trouble, both
in translating the novel version of *De vliegenvanger* and
in giving his numerous readings from it. He did so partly,
as we have seen, to help raise money for actors who were
out of work for refusing to enlist in the Kulturkammer,
and partly because he believed *The Moon Is Down* was
good propaganda and that he had a duty as a patriotic
Dutch actor to keep his war-weary fellow citizens mindful of the moral issues of the occupation.

People who had been to the theater to see German-
approved plays came to us and said, "Oh, it was a
lovely night; we forgot *everything*. It was as it had
been before." And I said, "I don't *want* you to forget
everything, and I don't want you to consider that this
was a night as it had been in the past, because the past
was *quite* different than what is going on now. You
should *never* forget it, and you should *never* be
unaware of it, of our conditions." And so I didn't

want to give performances even by myself in private houses for entertainment. I only wanted to do it as propaganda . . . and that was the only thing I wanted to do. . . . Our resistance was not so very important, but it was a good thing that it existed. We *needed* it, and I needed the feeling that something was . . . well, that we *tried* to do something, and I always said, if only you pick into [the Nazis] with pins, [even that] has its effect.

Shortly after the war, De Bizige Bij brought out a new edition of *De vliegenvanger* which, according to Sterneberg, "didn't look as nice" as the clandestine one printed earlier under the exigencies of occupation because publishers throughout Holland were forced by shortages to use inferior paper. De Bizige Bij transferred the rights to Sterneberg's translation to another Dutch publisher, Van Holkema and Warendorf. That firm eventually issued three more editions, the latest in 1977.[5] For the postwar editions Sterneberg received "a little bit of money," even though, since he had no legal rights to the novel, he had neither asked for nor expected any compensation.

Sterneberg and his fellow actors also decided to give dramatic performances of *The Moon Is Down* in Holland immediately following the liberation, this time using Steinbeck's own play version. At one of their rehearsals, however, they encountered new difficulty from an unexpected source—the Allies.

> We were preparing the show, and then came . . .
> the Canadian Army, and they wanted [our] theater
> for the entertainment of their soldiers. It was *terrible*.
> And we explained to them, [but] they weren't inter-
> ested at all, and we tried in our best English to make
> them understand that it was a thing they couldn't do.
> But oh, no, they wanted the building for their enter-
> tainment. Well, happily, the theater was too small,
> and they took a cinema [somewhere else].

That difficulty resolved, Sterneberg and his friends gave "many performances," and the play was a "big success."

Ferdinand Sterneberg retired from acting in 1969 except for occasional stints between that time and his death in 1987. These included a few appearances in television dramas and a return to the stage in 1981, when, at the age of seventy-nine, he played the role of the judge in Brian Clark's *Whose Life Is It, Anyhow?* What he remembered best about *The Moon Is Down* nearly forty years after he translated it was that although it is "a bit flattering" in its portrayal of the invaders (Sterneberg always referred to them as Germans), "the moral effect of it on the times was good." Somehow Steinbeck, with his "rather Latin mind," had perceived the feelings of the men and women living in a little country occupied by a much larger neighbor. In summarizing why he thought *The Moon Is Down* appealed so much to his own countrymen, Sterneberg said, "I think it was the way Steinbeck gave the mind of the people in such a small place."

5

France

TEINBECK was still writing *The Moon Is Down* in October 1941, when a young French artist named Jean Bruller put the finishing touches on a story soon to create a sensation in occupied France: *Le silence de la mer (The Silence of the Sea)*. Bruller, destined to become famous as Vercors, his nom de guerre, had been so disheartened by his country's surrender to the Germans in June 1940 that he had renounced his art and had withdrawn to a small village to work as a carpenter's helper. In those early days of occupation, intellectuals throughout the nation, particularly liberals and leftists, had resolved that although France had been conquered militarily, it must not be conquered spiritually. The great French ideals—respect for liberty and human dignity, for the traditions of Christianity and of the Encyclopedists, for the principles of the revolution—must be kept alive. In order to sustain their national ideals, these intellectuals founded numerous underground newspapers and journals, many of which sprang up soon after the Vichy capitulation.[1]

One such journal was the review *La Pensée Libre* (*Free Thought*). Its second number had just been published when the novelist Pierre de Lescure, who maintained contact with its editors, asked his old friend Bruller for help. De Lescure and the *Pensée Libre* editors had decided that the contents of their first two numbers were too overtly propagandistic. Numbers 3 and 4 of the review, scheduled for publication in the summer of 1941, were to be more literary. De Lescure and his friends sought to conduct intellectual business as usual, publishing French letters as though German authority did not exist, without a descent into merely political polemics. Thus de Lescure wanted Bruller to write a long story for the fourth issue of the *Pensée Libre*. Bruller accepted with misgivings, since he was a painter, not an author; but his doubts vanished when he delivered his manuscript to de Lescure in October.

De Lescure, moved by Bruller's story, wanted to publish it immediately after Bruller had made some revisions. During the few days required to effect those changes, however, the Gestapo raided the offices of the *Pensée Libre*, seized its supplies and unpublished material, and shut down its operations. Bruller, who was fortunately still in possession of his manuscript, then proposed to de Lescure that they print it themselves as a single volume. In discussing the matter, the two men determined to follow the publication of Bruller's piece with other single-volume works—in effect, to found a publishing house. De Lescure would be in charge of soliciting manuscripts, while Bruller would handle the printing and binding. Like other proud French intellectuals at the time, de Lescure and Bruller were eager to show the outside world that independent thought in France could not only survive German censorship but actually thrive under such suppression. And what better way to do that than by demonstrating that uncensored publications of fine quality could be turned out in Paris under the very nose of the Gestapo?

Bruller's first business was to find a printer. With some apprehension, he visited an old acquaintance, one M. Aulard, who owned a print shop in the city. To Bruller's relief, Aulard was willing to run the considerable risk of printing clandestine books; but after discussing the matter, they both realized that Aulard's business was too large. Too many employees could not be trusted absolutely. A few days later, however, Aulard sent Bruller to a young printer named Oudeville, who ran a one-man shop between two mortuaries in the Boulevard de l'Hôpital. Just across the boulevard was the Hôpital de la Pitié, then serving as a German military hospital. Aulard furnished Oudeville with an attractive Garamond type, and Oudeville worked on Bruller's story between his regular jobs. Bruller visited Oudeville's shop frequently to oversee the printing, since Oudeville specialized in wedding and funeral cards and had no experience in setting full pages. Even under such conditions of close cooperation, Oudeville did not know that the Jean Bruller who had brought him the manuscript and had overseen its publication was actually its author, the Vercors who would become the most famous writer of the French Resistance.

Oudeville delayed the printing of the title page and cover until last because Bruller and de Lescure had not yet settled on a name for their "publishing house." When the decision could be postponed no longer, Bruller, de Lescure, and some colleagues proposed and rejected several names, among them Underground Publications and Catacomb Publications. Finally Bruller himself hit upon one that sounded just right: Éditions de Minuit (Midnight Editions).

By the time Oudeville finished printing *Le silence de la mer*, Bruller had already contacted a childhood friend, Yvonne Paraf, later known by her nom de guerre, Yvonne Desvignes, who had agreed to stitch the pages together after he collated them. But another matter remained to be settled. Because Bruller and de Lescure had decided to accept no foreign financial aid for their clandestine publications (the operations must be perceived as entirely French), Bruller had to find funds to defray initial expenses. He had little difficulty. His first inquiry resulted in a guarantee of three thousand francs.

Despite their success in launching an illegal publishing operation in occupied Paris, it had taken Bruller and de Lescure two months to bring out *Le silence de la mer.* They knew the process would have to be accelerated considerably if they were to achieve the volume they had envisioned. The problem was solved when Oudeville found a linotypist named Roulois, who worked in his home in the rue Friant. Roulois was able to reduce to twelve days the time required for publication of the next volume from Éditions de Minuit, Jacques Maritain's *À travers le désastre* (*Through the Disaster*). Oudeville's collaboration with the Éditions, however, soon came to an end when he was obliged to hire a helper whom he did not know well enough to trust. But by then Aulard had made arrangements with his foreman and two old friends to print future volumes in his shop on Sunday when no other employees would be present. From the time he began to print for the Éditions de Minuit until the liberation, Aulard worked on every volume it published. Among those volumes was *The Moon Is Down.*

By October 1943 Éditions de Minuit was well known throughout occupied France. *Le silence de la mer* had created a sensation not only at home but in England and America as well, where editions had appeared in both French and English. *Life* magazine had carried a complete translation. Clearly, French letters were alive and well. The Éditions had also managed to publish more than ten other volumes since its establishment. Yvonne Paraf-Desvignes, who in addition to her stitching and binding distributed books all over Paris by motorbike and held staff meetings nearly every week in her apartment, was to assume yet another duty: that of translator.

Through intermediaries in Vichy, Mme. Paraf-Desvignes acquired a copy of a Swedish edition (in English) of *The Moon Is Down*. She knew that a French translation of the novel had already been published by Marguerat Editions in Lausanne, Switzerland, earlier in 1943. But she also knew that that version, entitled *Nuits sans lune* (*Moonless Nights*), had been censored by the Swiss government, apprehensive about displeasing its German neighbor. Deleted were Steinbeck's references in *The Moon Is Down* to England, to the war in Russia, and to the occupation of Belgium by the aggressor army twenty years after a previous occupation, references which left no doubt about the identity of the unnamed country to which that army belonged. Because of these and other omissions from the Swiss edition, Mme. Paraf-Desvignes, encouraged by Vercors, undertook a new translation. The well-known poet Paul Eluard, one of a group who met regularly at Mme. Paraf-Desvignes's apartment, chose the new French title: *Nuits noires* (*Black Nights*).[2]

Like *Le silence de la mer*, *Nuits noires* enjoyed an "immense and incontestable" success among the French literary public after its release on 29 February 1944. Printed in an edition of nearly 1,500 copies, the largest undertaken by Éditions de Minuit during the occupation, it was celebrated in the press and in all the clandestine reviews. According to procedures by then well established by the Éditions, the small paperbacks (they measured 6 ½ by 4 ½ inches) were distributed in France through a network of writers and sold in bookstores under the counter—at some risk. Proceeds from the sales were turned over to the National Committee of Writers, which used the funds to help families of patriotic printers and typographers who had been shot or deported.

Readers in occupied France responded enthusiastically to *Nuits noires* for many of the same reasons they had earlier hailed *Le silence de la mer*. In fact, as Albert Gerard has pointed out, the two works have much in common. "In [them] you find the same gift of human sympathy, the same comprehension of the individual, of his problems and of his destiny." And, like *Le silence de la mer*, *The Moon Is Down* was said to avoid "the facile flaw of propaganda in black and white."[3] Indeed, Steinbeck's honesty, manifested in *The Moon Is Down* by his eschewing the stereotypes of propaganda, was a literary virtue already recognized by French intellectuals, many of whom were familiar with Steinbeck's earlier works. That perception of Steinbeck's basic honesty as a writer paved the way for the immediate acceptance of *Nuits noires*.

Jean-Paul Sartre observed shortly after the war that the novels of Steinbeck, "the most severe critic of the capitalistic form of production in the United States," in 1944 were constant reminders to Frenchmen of American liberty. "We knew that in Germany such a book as *The Grapes of Wrath* could never have been published." When the Nazis, hoping to score propaganda points against the United States, allowed the publication in France of Steinbeck's *In Dubious Battle*, and when the owner of a collaborationist bookstore in Paris arranged in one of his windows copies of that novel next to photographs depicting scenes of violence in America, Frenchmen smashed the windows and two policemen had to be dispatched to guard the display. Later, says Sartre, when the Americans broke through the Nazi line in Normandy, the Germans were preparing to distribute a French translation of *The Grapes of Wrath*, published by a Belgian collaborationist editor. Ironically, those preparations occurred at the same time the Éditions de Minuit was circulating *Nuits noires*, "which seemed to us all like a message from fighting America to the European

FRANCE

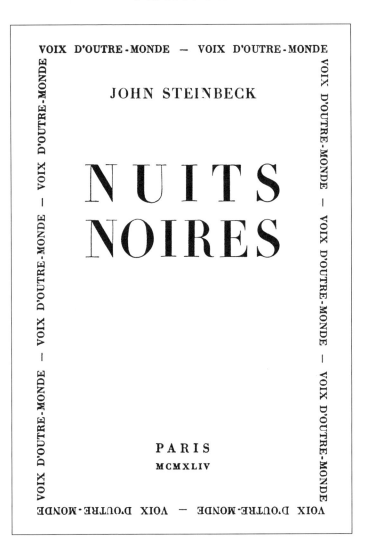

Cover of *Nuits noires*. (*Courtesy of Éditions de Minuit*)

underground." Hence, Sartre concludes, "the most rebellious, perhaps, of your writers held the ambiguous position of being acclaimed at the same time by the collaborationists and by the underground."[4]

The Moon Is Down was popular in occupied France for the same basic reason that it was popular in occupied Scandinavia and in Holland: Steinbeck somehow sensed how the Norwegians, the Danes, the Dutch, and the French felt about living under the Nazis. Jacques Debû-Bridel, one of the founders of the Éditions de Minuit as well as its historian, marvels that a novel written "across the Atlantic by a man removed by more than five thousand kilometers from oppressed Europe" could be such a "masterpiece of understanding." Yvonne Paraf-Desvignes suggests in her translator's note to *Nuits noires* that it is Steinbeck's allegiance to higher verities that accounts for the novel's appeal. Its "spiritual breath," she says, "is one of the historical truths of our time."[5]

In postwar France, as in other previously occupied European countries, the publication of *The Moon Is Down* in regular trade editions immediately after the liberation affirmed the significance of its earlier role and the high regard in which it was held. On 25 May 1945, the Éditions de Minuit published *Nuits noires* in a volume which was "in every way faithful to that one published by the Éditions de Minuit under the occupation." That volume was in fact one of several in a collection of works which constituted the first public edition of the Éditions de Minuit. Of the 5,325 copies produced in this edition of *Nuits noires*, 3,735 were intended for distribution in France, 1,590 for export. All were numbered copies. Most were printed on vellum, some on *pure fil* from the Papeteries de France, a few on Madagascar paper from the Navarre Paperies.[6] The editors of the Éditions de Minuit did not need to produce such elegant volumes in order to prove to themselves and to the outside world that French letters could withstand the rigors of Nazi occupation. Such volumes did serve, however, as resplendent declarations of triumph.

6

Other Countries

HE WARTIME publication of *The Moon Is Down* was not limited to America and occupied Europe. Steinbeck's British publisher, Heinemann, brought out the first edition of the novel in England in 1942, and a "Middle East Edition" the following year. The English Theatre Guild printed Steinbeck's dramatic version in 1943, and on 8 June of that year the play opened at the Whitehall Theatre.

At least one translation was apparently published and distributed within the Axis itself. In May 1957 Steinbeck wrote from Florence to his old friend and editor Pascal Covici, mentioning that at a cocktail party he had met an Italian man who had been a fugitive from both Mussolini and Hitler.

> He told me that during the war he came on a little thin book printed on onion skin paper which so exactly described Italy that he translated and ran off

five hundred copies on a mimeograph. It was *The Moon Is Down*. He said it went everywhere in the resistance and requests came in for it from all over even though possession was an automatic death sentence. And do you remember the attacks on it at home from our bellicose critics?[1]

This writer's inquiries to Italian academicians, authors, publishers, librarians, and resistance leaders uncovered no information about a wartime clandestine edition of *The Moon Is Down* in Italy. The publication of three regular Italian-language editions around the time the war ended, however, would suggest unusual interest in the novel in that country. The earliest of these, *La luna e tramontata* (*The Moon Has Gone Down*), translated by Luciana Peverelli, was published in Rome by Editoriale Romana in 1944, the same year that Heinemann and Zsolnay published in London a version entitled *Notte senza luna* (*Night without Moon*), with the translator's name not given. In 1945 yet another Italian edition, translated by Giorgio Monicelli, was published in Milan by Mondadori under the title *La luna tramonta* (*The Setting Moon*).

In Sweden there was great interest in *The Moon Is Down*, aroused by anguish over the suffering under Nazi authority of fellow Scandinavians in Norway and Denmark and by fear of sharing such a fate, should the Germans decide to extend their control over all of

Scandinavia. The possibility of such an invasion, incidentally, had prevented Steinbeck's Swedish friend Bo Beskow from joining him in Mexico. According to Beskow, the two had planned to collaborate on a book about that country; Beskow was to have provided the illustrations for Steinbeck's text.[2] In 1942, roughly two years after the Germans overran Denmark and Norway, three different editions were published in Sweden: Nils Lie's Norwegian translation, *Natt uten måne*, printed by Åhlén and Åkerlunds and intended, as we have seen earlier, for clandestine distribution in Norway; a Swedish translation by Thorsten Jonsson entitled *Månen har gått ned* (*The Moon Has Gone Down*), issued by Bonnier (a conglomerate embracing Åhlén and Åkerlunds); and an English language edition put out by another Bonnier affiliate, the Continental Book Company, in its Clipper Book Series, which must have been the edition Mme. Paraf-Desvignes used when she made her French translation. A play version apparently had a successful run in Sweden. In March 1943 Steinbeck wrote his old friend Toby Street, "According to the Swedish radio, Moon, which opened two nights ago in Stockholm, is a smash hit."[3]

Far to the south during 1942 and 1943, the Swiss were as worried about a Nazi takeover as the Swedes. The president of the Swiss Federal Council lamented that his people were "a pigeon's egg in the hand of a gorilla."[4]

Mindful of their precarious situation, Swiss officials frequently censored publications and theatrical performances likely to offend the Germans. Despite Swiss fears of incurring Nazi displeasure, however, two editions of *The Moon Is Down* found their way into print in the confederation in 1943: the expurgated French language version discussed earlier, *Nuits sans lune*, translated by Marvéde-Fischer and published in Lausanne by Marguerat; and a German language version, *Der Mond ging unter* (*The Moon Went Down*), translated by Anna Katharina Rehmann-Salten (later Wyler-Salten) and published in Zürich by Humanitas Verlag. Rehmann-Salten, the only daughter of Felix Salten (best known as the author of *Bambi*), was born in Vienna and had been an actress, mostly under the direction of Max Reinhart.[5] When Hitler came to power, she emigrated from Berlin, where she had been living, to Zürich. There, in the fall of 1942, she worked on her German translation of *The Moon Is Down* and, like Ferdinand Sterneberg of Holland, on her own dramatization of the novel. She completed both in November.

Because the Nazis at that time were still on the offensive in Europe and because Switzerland was encircled by German armies, Swiss apprehensions that their country would suffer the same fate as Steinbeck's "Norway" were higher than at any other period in the war. For this reason, even the Zürich theater, the Schauspielhaus, then "the cultural center of resistance against Nazism," at first refused to touch Rehmann-Salten's dramatic adaptation. After the play opened to enthusiastic audiences at a theater in Basel, however, the Zürich Schauspielhaus capitulated, and *The Moon Is Down* enjoyed there a lengthy and highly acclaimed run of around two hundred performances. According to Zürich professor Heinrich Straumann, it was "one of the greatest successes of the theatres of Switzerland during the war years."[6] Together, the novel and the dramatic versions of Rehmann-Salten's translation helped strengthen Swiss resolve against Nazi intimidation.

In the Soviet Union, *The Moon Is Down* was the best-known work of contemporary American literature during the war.[7] Two Russian-language versions of the novel were serialized in Soviet magazines in 1943: one, a complete translation by N. Volzhina, appeared in *Znamya*; the other, consisting of excerpts translated by A. Belyayev, in *Ogonyok*.[8] Although Soviet critics were favorably disposed toward Steinbeck at the time because he had depicted the abuses of capitalism in his proletarian novels of the thirties, these critics were virtually unanimous in their criticism of *The Moon Is Down*. Their most common complaints echoed those voiced in the United States a year earlier by critics such as James

Thurber and Clifton Fadiman. Steinbeck's "humanizing" of the Nazis showed that he had only "a foggy understanding of Fascist mentality," and his portrayal of the resistance of the citizens of the mythical village of the novel was vague and unrealistic. According to Deming Brown, only one Soviet critic strongly endorsed *The Moon Is Down*.[9]

But the survival of the Soviet Union still hung in the balance in 1943, and Russian critics were reserving their praise for war literature which would serve them more unambiguously as morale-boosting propaganda for the Allied cause. Besides, the Germans had been especially savage in the Soviet Union. Official Nazi racial policy had designated the Russian people *Untermenschen*, or subhumans, and Nazi soldiers, accordingly, had brutalized the populace. Small wonder that in a land where German atrocities were committed on an inconceivable scale, Steinbeck's "Nazi" invaders seemed airy figments of a naive foreigner's imagination.

Far to the east, however, in another besieged land, *The Moon Is Down* seems to have served as antifascist propaganda no less effectively than in western Europe at the time. The first publication of a Chinese-language version of Steinbeck's novel was in *New China* magazine. Originally published in Shanghai by the Zhong Hua (China) Book Company, *New China* had ceased production at the beginning of the Sino-Japanese War. Later, the magazine moved its operations to China's wartime capital of Chungking, in Szechwan Province.

One of the editors of the revived publication was a professor of Chinese literature, Chien Gochuen. Sometime late in 1942 Professor Chien procured a copy of the English edition of *The Moon Is Down* through the British press Attaché's office in Chungking. Recognizing its value as anti-Japanese propaganda, Chien decided to translate it into Chinese. Beginning in January 1943, Chien's translation appeared under his nom de guerre, Ch'in Ko Chuan, in the first seven issues of the Chungking-based *New China* magazine. Chien's pseudonym, which means "The Chinese Warship," is written with three Chinese characters that have almost the same sound as Chien's real name.[10] *New China* published ten thousand copies of each of those issues— an extraordinary number for that time, considering the formidable wartime restrictions in China. Shortly after printing the last of the seven installments, Zhong Hua compiled them in a single edition which it then distributed throughout the country.

For the single-volume version, Professor Chien, aware that Steinbeck's title was taken from Shakespeare, searched for a phrase from Chinese poetry which would capture its nuances. Eventually he settled upon a famous poem entitled "Anchored at Night by Maple Bridge," whose first line furnished his title. The entire poem reads as follows:

> Moon sets, crows caw, sky is full of frost;
> River maples, fishing boat lights break through my
> troubled sleep.
> Beyond the city of Su-chou lies Han Shan monastery:
> At midnight the clang of the bell reaches the traveller's
> boat.[11]

Written by Chang Chi during the golden age of Chinese literature under the Tang Dynasty (A.D. 618–907), "Anchored at Night by Maple Bridge" proved a highly appropriate source for Chien for two reasons: it suggests darkness—spiritual as well as actual—but the darkness just before daybreak, and it is a favorite of the Chinese people.

No records remain of the number of copies Zhong Hua published of Professor Chien's single-volume translation of *The Moon Is Down*. Moreover, Zhong Hua of Beijing knows of "no single . . . copy in existence today"; Professor Chien knows of only one: the copy he kept for himself. But both Chien (who later moved to the United States) and a spokesman for Zhong Hua (which is still in business in Beijing) remember that it and the magazine installment publication that preceded it were popular and effective propaganda. In the words of the Zhong Hua spokesman, "The patriotic eagerness of [Steinbeck's] characters to resist their conquerors motivated the Chinese people to resist Japanese invasion and to defend China against Japanese imperialism."

7

Conclusion

N JUNE 1942, three months after the raging controversy over *The Moon Is Down* had begun, Stanley Edgar Hyman wrote in the *Antioch Review* that the effect of the novel as propaganda "will probably be somewhere along the line from the useless to the downright dangerous. No book that bases its hopes for the conquered peoples on such physical weapons as dynamite and chocolate, such mental weapons as sabotage so intelligent and inventive that it need never be organized, and such spiritual weapons as a God that is always on the side of the freer battalions, is likely to help in the war effort." While he was echoing critics who had already made similar prognostications, Hyman at least avoided smug certainty by acknowledging that the jury was still out. "Whether in actual value the book will do more to inspire or to disarm the struggle against the Axis is still debatable."[1]

By the time the war ended three years later, interest

in the debate had long since waned. No one in 1945 was interested in digging up the bones of an old literary feud, one by then politically irrelevant. Despite a few early testimonies of its success, most notably the decoration awarded Steinbeck by the king of Norway in 1946, there was no recognition of the full breadth and depth of the enthusiasm which *The Moon Is Down* had aroused in the recently liberated nations of western Europe, where the impact it had made reveals most convincingly its success as propaganda. Most of the evidence of that success remained scattered, sketchy, or anecdotal.

Today we have a sufficiently complete picture of its career as propaganda to conclude simply and certainly that Hyman, along with James Thurber, Clifton Fadiman, and the other American critics who had predicted the utter failure of *The Moon Is Down* as propaganda, were entirely wrong. The unusual popularity of the novel in countries where it was circulated for that purpose is clearly demonstrated in several ways: by the dedication of those who translated, printed, and distributed it at considerable risk, sometimes—as in Denmark—under the very nose of the Gestapo; by the impressive number of editions and copies published both during the occupation on makeshift machinery and under taxing conditions as well as after the war by recently liberated publishing houses; and by the testimonies of former members of the anti-Nazi resistance and others who had played a role in its dissemination or who had witnessed firsthand its power to inspire and to reassure.

Several questions arise beyond the obvious conclusion that Steinbeck had been right and his critics wrong in projecting how *The Moon Is Down* would play as propaganda in occupied Europe. Why were the hostile American critics so mistaken, and how do we account for the discrepancy between their reaction to the novel and that of the Europeans? Basically, why did the American critics fail to see what so appealed to the Europeans? And finally, what does the stunning European success of *The Moon Is Down* tell us about Steinbeck the writer?

In the third chapter of his postwar essay *What Is Literature?* Jean-Paul Sartre examines the fundamental question of audience: For whom does one write? His basic contention is that since "all works of the mind contain within themselves the image of the reader for whom they are intended," we can have no true understanding of a literary work unless we know who an author is writing for. To illustrate his point, Sartre recalls that Vercors's *Silence of the Sea* had a hostile reception in New York, London, and Algiers among French émigrés, who in some instances went so far as to accuse Vercors of collaboration. In occupied France, on the other hand, *The Silence of the Sea* was the most popular and perhaps the most effective anti-German literature produced during the war. There, says Sartre, Vercors's aim was perfectly clear. "Nobody doubted the author's intentions or the efficacy of his writing; he was writing for us." What the émigrés objected to was Vercors's portrayal of the German invaders as human beings, often intelligent, if misguided, and frequently polite and likable. The émigrés preferred the Manichean simplicities of most contemporary Anglo-Saxon propaganda, which presented German soldiers as ogres. Such a portrayal, Sartre argues, would have been laughable to the people of Vichy France in 1941. Those who experienced the occupation and who had daily contact with the enemy saw that there were good men and bad in the ranks of their conquerors. Any propaganda which grossly distorted that reality would have failed among those who knew the truth.[2]

Sartre's explanation of the discrepancy between the response to *The Silence of the Sea* from the people of occupied France and that from Frenchmen living abroad at the time applies as well to *The Moon Is Down*. During the furor which arose in the United States just after the publication of that novel, the point of fiercest controversy was Steinbeck's treatment of his fictional Germans. Was he being soft on these characters by portraying them as human beings rather than as stereotypical Huns, and would such an allegedly sympathetic depiction of the enemy have a demoralizing effect on the populace of occupied Europe—people whose spirits Steinbeck hoped to lift? As we have seen, Steinbeck's harshest critics on this score were Americans far removed from the action. When James Thurber, perhaps the most strident detractor of *The Moon Is Down*, wondered what the people of Poland would make of the novel, he was implying that Poles—or by extension, any Europeans experiencing the indignities and brutalities of the Nazi New Order—would shake their heads in disbelief at Steinbeck's ignorance of the realities of German occupation. The author who had recently written so sensitively about dispossessed Okies had this time missed the mark and missed it badly.

Steinbeck, of course, had been right on target. By avoiding propagandistic rant in depicting his "German" soldiers, he, like Vercors, was revealing not only shrewd psychological perception but also a respect for the sophistication of his European audience. It is Steinbeck's much-criticized humanization of his "German" soldiers, in fact, which Roy S. Simmonds says largely accounts for its "true importance" during the war, since that humanization "was the very element, together with Steinbeck's moving depiction of the quiet courage of Mayor Orden, that gave much-needed encouragement and impetus to the resistance fighters in the occupied countries."[3]

Steinbeck's accomplishment in reaching his particular European audience seems all the more remarkable when we consider that, unlike Vercors, he was not on the scene. Vercors was writing as a Frenchman, from personal experience, voicing feelings which he and his compatriots were compelled by their sorry circumstances to confront. But Steinbeck was over three thousand miles away. While it is true that during his wartime government service he had associated with refugees from occupied Europe and had presumably acquired from them a reasonably accurate picture of the situation there, it is quite another matter for him or for any other writer removed from the scene to infer from such secondhand details the deepest feelings of the inhabitants.

It was Steinbeck's intuitive recognition of their feelings and his ability to express them which seems to have most impressed the Europeans. In the interviews cited in earlier chapters—interviews of those who had actually experienced the duress and ignominy of defeat and occupation by the Germans and who were moreover familiar with the reception of *The Moon Is Down* in their various countries—the explanation of its popularity recurring more frequently than any other is that Steinbeck had somehow known exactly how they had felt during their ordeal. Steinbeck "had insight . . . especially into [our] reaction against the ones who took over the country"; "Steinbeck gave the mind of the people in such a small place"; *The Moon Is Down* fed our "hunger for sympathy"; it brought out "things . . . hidden within the people . . . living in a small country"; "[our] feelings were all there in the book: there were our problems, our hopes, our sorrows"; *The Moon Is Down* is a "masterpiece of understanding." Steinbeck's perception of the Europeans' psychological and spiritual needs arising from their peculiar circumstances meant that for them his novel was an uncommonly direct and intensely personal communication. Shortly after the war Donald Weeks observed that *The Moon Is Down* is "limited by its occasional character as a novel of the war."[4] In fact, it was the very nature of that work as an occasional piece— a work addressing urgent and immediate issues—which accounts for much of its impact upon Steinbeck's wartime European audience.

That Steinbeck was able to imagine those feelings should come as no surprise. What readers in occupied Europe found most appealing in *The Moon Is Down* only serves to remind us of what prewar readers all over the world had recognized as one of Steinbeck's major strengths: his empathy with the downtrodden and his compassionate understanding of the underdog. It is akin to a quality which Frederick J. Hoffman finds in Steinbeck's novels of the 1930s: a "remarkable, almost uncanny ability to meet the intellectual and emotional needs of a depression-trained reading public."[5] *The Moon Is Down* demonstrated that Steinbeck's special sense of audience was not limited to the people of his own country. Part of the secret of his appeal to his foreign audience is doubtless revealed in John Ditsky's explanation of how Steinbeck avoided the dangers of writing about what he did not actually know. He simply assumed "that people, for the most part, are the same wherever they live."[6] During his visit to Norway in 1946, Steinbeck alluded to his use of such a technique. On several occasions, former members of the resistance asked him, "How did you know what we were doing, all those tricks we played on the Germans? We thought that it all was secret." Steinbeck's reply was, "I guessed. I put myself in your place and thought what I would do."[7]

In addition to providing his European audiences the reassurance that a world-famous writer understood their reactions to the traumas of occupation, Steinbeck also offered them a reaffirmation of cherished ideas and traditions which had been abruptly taken from them and whose very survival must have seemed at times threatened with extinction. Against the confusing polemics of war, the shabby political compromises of well-meaning governments scrambling to salvage security for their people, and the frustrating suppression of truth by occupation authorities, Steinbeck reiterated the basic val-

CONCLUSION

ues of Western civilization: freedom, the worth of the individual, and the collective power which derives from free individuals with common commitments.

Steinbeck's villagers are exemplars. They react to unprovoked invasion and the usurpation of their rights in the way we would expect of free people anywhere. Bewildered at first by surprise attack and overwhelmed by the well-organized military power of a totalitarian state, they eventually discover within themselves the greatest strength of a democracy: the strength of free individuals united under leaders like Mayor Orden who are merely upholders of common values. Steinbeck's understanding of that strength is supported by the most realistic of political observers, Machiavelli, who believed that democratic states are the most difficult to subdue. In cities and principalities which "have been accustomed to living freely under their own laws," he says in *The Prince*, "there is more life, more hatred, a greater desire for revenge; [their citizens'] memory of their ancient liberty does not and cannot let them rest."[8]

In Steinbeck's reassertion of basic Western values and ideals, he was consistent with views he had developed in his earlier writing regarding the human being as a biological organism—views which Edmund Wilson had claimed in 1941 constituted for Steinbeck an artistically stultifying preoccupation.[9] According to Jackson Benson, it is from those biological views of human behavior that Steinbeck derives his meaning in *The Moon Is Down*: the idea that democratic states are inherently stronger than totalitarian ones, that "'herd men' cannot over the long haul compete with free men." As Mayor Orden tells Colonel Lanser near the end of the novel, "Free men cannot start a war, but once it is started, they can fight on in defeat. Herd men, followers of a leader, cannot do that, and so it is always the herd men who win battles and the free men who win wars."[10] That idea, says Benson, was not in Steinbeck's mind a matter of "patriotic sentimentality," as Thurber believed, but "an unsentimental biological fact."[11]

Whatever the biological underpinnings of *The Moon Is Down*, it is obviously more for what was perceived as its artful championing of threatened values than for any implicit espousal of scientific social theory that the work enjoyed its success during the war. According to Swiss professor Heinrich Straumann, it was Steinbeck's attention to the "basic value of solidarity ... connected with the traditional ideals of freedom, personal dignity, and local self-government" that made *The Moon Is Down* for the European reader "the most powerful piece of propaganda ever written to help a small democratic country to resist totalitarian aggression and occupation."[12] That same attention to traditional ideas would also account for another of its features not characteristic of most works of propaganda: its remarkable staying power. Roy Simmonds has observed that "of all the works of propagandist war fiction written during the years 1939–1945 it is one of the mere handful that have survived and are still being read and discussed."[13]

That staying power is attested to by the appearance of no fewer than seventy-six editions between 1945 and 1989. Besides the twenty-one editions in English (eleven American and ten British), there have been six in Danish; five each in Dutch and Spanish (three published in Spain, one in Mexico, and one "South American edition"); four each in Hungarian and French (three of *Nuit sans lune* and one of *Nuits noires* reprinted in Belgium); three each in Turkish, German (Switzerland), Chinese (three different translations—one published in Shanghai before the Communist takeover, and two in Taiwan), and Japanese (two different translations); two each in Arabic (Egypt), Swedish, Italian, Portuguese (one in Portugal and one in Brazil), Korean, Urdu (India), and Greek; and one each in Slovak (Yugoslavia), Polish, Persian (Iran), Burmese, and Norwegian.[14]

Since the war, many scholars, among them some Steinbeck specialists, have pointed to weaknesses in *The Moon Is Down*: wooden characters, lack of a rich texture, a straining after effect, and an obtrusive didacticism, to name those most commonly cited. Some of these may be attributed to the haste with which the work was written (Steinbeck wanted to complete it while it could still do some good), while others are simply characteristic of novels of ideas in which characters serve mainly as vehicles for those ideas and in which social interaction, meant to fulfill a similar function, may seem stilted and artificial.

Certainly it is difficult to deny that, judged by purely literary standards, *The Moon Is Down* is not among Steinbeck's best novels. Indeed there is evidence that Steinbeck himself considered it little more than a patriotic duty, an assignment written at the behest of one of the government agencies he worked for during the war.[15] It is, moreover, an unassuming work whose transparency of purpose makes it particularly vulnerable to criticism in our age of sophisticated metafiction. But few books have demonstrated more triumphantly the power of ideas against brute military strength, and few books in recent times have spoken with such reassurance to so many people of different countries and cultures. To readers affected most directly by the terror and despair of Nazi occupation, *The Moon Is Down* was an inspiriting statement of faith that despite the darkness of their hour, freedom and decency would return. That power to inspire—its greatest virtue for millions of victims of Nazi oppression—remains today its signal distinction. After the lights had gone out all over Europe for the second time in our century, John Steinbeck's modest novel was a beacon of hope in a seemingly hopeless night.

Notes

1. PUBLICATION
AND AMERICAN RECEPTION

1. John Steinbeck, *Steinbeck: A Life in Letters*, ed. Elaine Steinbeck and Robert Wallsten (New York: Viking, 1975) 205, 207.

2. Steinbeck, *Life in Letters* 206.

3. Steinbeck, *Life in Letters* 206–07.

4. John Steinbeck, "About Ed Ricketts," *The Log from the Sea of Cortez*, by John Steinbeck and Ed Ricketts (New York: Viking, 1951) lviii–lxii.

5. John Steinbeck, "The Secret Weapon We Were Afraid to Use," *Colliers* 10 Jan. 1953: 9–10.

6. John Steinbeck, "Letters to Alicia," *Weekend with Newsday* 11 Dec. 1965: 3W.

7. John Steinbeck, "Reflections on a Lunar Eclipse," *Herald Tribune* [New York] 6 Oct. 1963, Sunday *Book Week* section: 3.

8. Steinbeck, "Reflections on a Lunar Eclipse" 3.

9. Thomas Kiernan, in *The Intricate Music: A Biography of John Steinbeck* (Boston: Little, 1979) 254–56, offers another expla-

nation of Steinbeck's motivation for writing *The Moon Is Down*. According to Kiernan, Steinbeck urgently needed money. By the time he had finished *Sea of Cortez* in June 1941, he had made up his mind to divorce his first wife, Carol Henning, and to marry Gwen Conger. His attorney, longtime friend Toby Street, advised him that his freedom would cost him all the money he had. According to Kiernan, Steinbeck believed that his next work might be more lucrative if, like *Of Mice and Men*, it yielded income both as a novel and as a play. In fairness to Steinbeck, it should be pointed out that only a short time later, in 1942, he gave all royalties from *Bombs Away*, the work he wrote for the air force, to the Air Forces Aid Society Trust Fund. The movie rights alone totaled $250,000.

10. Steinbeck, "Reflections on a Lunar Eclipse" 3.

11. Steinbeck, "Reflections on a Lunar Eclipse" 3.

12. Jackson J. Benson, *The True Adventures of John Steinbeck, Writer* (New York: Viking, 1984) 491–92.

13. Steinbeck, *Life in Letters* 238.

14. Benson, *True Adventures*, 487–88.

15. Lewis Gannett, introduction, "John Steinbeck's Way of Writing," *The Portable Steinbeck*, ed. Pascal Covici, 1969 ed. (New York: Viking 1943) xxvi.

16. Scholars who have mentioned such a meeting between Steinbeck and Donovan and who have documented that detail have cited either Gannett or another scholar who acknowledged Gannett as the source. Even though there is no reason to question Gannett's claim, the historical record unfortunately sheds no light on it. The official records of the Office of Strategic Services contain

no suggestion of any contact between Steinbeck and Donovan (Larry R. Strawderman, letter to the author [response to a Freedom of Information Act request], 20 July 1982). Neither do Donovan biographers Thomas F. Troy and Richard Dunlop, wartime OSS operatives William E. Colby, Richard Helms, and Kermit Roosevelt, or close Donovan associate Archibald MacLeish recall ever hearing of a Steinbeck-Donovan meeting (letters to the author from Thomas F. Troy, 20 Jan. 1982; Richard Dunlop, 31 Mar. 1981; William E. Colby, 30 Mar. 1981; Richard Helms, 23 Mar. 1981; Kermit Roosevelt, 20 Mar. 1981; and Archibald MacLeish, 8 Apr. 1981). Troy says that Donovan saw so many people during the time in question that even if a Steinbeck-Donovan meeting was official (which it may well not have been), it could have gone unrecorded.

17. Anthony Cave Brown, *The Last Hero: Wild Bill Donovan* (New York: Times, 1982) 170–73.

18. John Chamberlain, "Books of the Times," rev. of *The Moon Is Down*, *New York Times* 6 Mar. 1942: 19.

19. Clifton Fadiman, "Two Ways to Win the War," rev. of *The Moon Is Down*, *New Yorker* 7 Mar. 1942: 52.

20. R. L. Duffus, "John Steinbeck's Heroic Tale '*The Moon Is Down*' Is a Narrative of Great Dramatic Intensity," rev. of *The Moon Is Down*, *New York Times Book Review* 8 Mar. 1942, sec. 6: 1.

21. John Gunther, rev. of *The Moon Is Down*, *Herald Tribune Books* [New York] 8 Mar. 1942: 1.

22. "Viewpoint of Victory," rev. of *The Moon Is Down, Time* 9 Mar. 1942: 84.

23. James Thurber, "What Price Conquest?" rev. of *The Moon Is Down, New Republic* 16 Mar. 1942: 370.

24. "Mr. Steinbeck, Friends and Foes," editorial, *New Republic* 30 Mar. 1942: 413.

25. Marshall A. Best, letter, *New Republic* 30 Mar. 1942: 431.

26. James Thurber, letter, *New Republic* 30 Mar. 1942: 431.

27. "Polish Refugee," letter, *New Republic* 30 Mar. 1942: 431–32.

28. Clifton Fadiman, "Steinbeck Again," rev. of *The Moon Is Down, New Yorker* 4 Apr. 1942: 63.

29. Frank G. Nelson, letter, *New Republic* 13 Apr. 1942: 495.

30. Hans Olav, letter, *New Republic* 4 May 1942: 607.

31. "Notes on Books and Authors," *New York Times*, 28 Apr. 1942: 19.

32. Lewis Gannett, "Books and Things," *Herald Tribune* [New York] 4 May 1942: 11.

33. "The Moon Is Halfway Down," editorial, *New Republic* 18 May 1942: 657.

34. Kiernan 260.

35. "'The Moon Is Down': Steinbeck Extols Humanity at War," rev. of *The Moon Is Down, Life* 6 Apr. 1942: 32.

36. Steinbeck, *Life in Letters* 242.

37. Kiernan 261–62.

38. Warren French, "*The Moon Is Down*: John Steinbeck's 'Times,'" *Steinbeck Quarterly* Summer–Fall 1978: 81.

39. Joseph R. Millichap, *Steinbeck and Film* (New York: Ungar, 1983) 60, 69–71.

40. Allan M. Winkler, *The Politics of Propaganda: The Office of War Information, 1942–1945* (New Haven: Yale University Press, 1978) 59.

41. Jackson J. Benson, *Looking for Steinbeck's Ghost* (Norman: University of Oklahoma Press, 1988) 192.

42. John Steinbeck, "My Short Novels," *Steinbeck and His Critics*, ed. E. W. Tedlock, Jr., and C. V. Wicker (Albuquerque: University of New Mexico Press, 1957) 39.

43. Steinbeck, "Reflections on a Lunar Eclipse" 3.

44. Steinbeck, *Life in Letters* 244.

45. Quentin Reynolds, *The Curtain Rises* (New York: Random, 1944) 263.

46. Elaine Steinbeck, letter to the author, 1 Nov. 1979.

47. Steinbeck, *Life in Letters* 590.

48. Steinbeck, "Reflections on a Lunar Eclipse" 3.

49. Elaine Steinbeck, letter to the author.

2. NORWAY

1. Steinbeck, *Life in Letters* 767–68.

2. Adrian H. Goldstone and John R. Payne, *John Steinbeck:*

A Bibliographical Catalogue of the Adrian H. Goldstone Collection (Austin: University of Texas Humanities Research Center, 1974) 176.

3. John Steinbeck, *The Moon Is Down: Play in Two Parts* (London: English Theatre Guild, 1943) 6.

4. John Steinbeck, Forlagets efterskrift, *Maanen er gaaet ned* (n.p.: Frit Nordisk Forlag, 1943 [1944]) [70].

5. Budd Schulberg, "John Steinbeck: A Lion in Winter," *The Four Seasons of Success* (Garden City, NY: Doubleday, 1972) 187–97. Rpt. in *Conversations with John Steinbeck*, ed. Thomas Fensch (Jackson: University Press of Mississippi, 1988) 109.

6. Steinbeck, "Reflections on a Lunar Eclipse" 3.

7. Oddvar Aas, letter to the author, 18 July 1981.

8. Arne Skouen, letter to the author, 10 Aug. 1981.

9. Aas, letter to the author.

10. Skouen, letter to the author.

11. Skouen, letter to the author.

12. John Dahl, personal interview, 22 May 1981.

13. Gordon Hølmebakk, personal interview, 21 May 1981.

14. William Ebenstein, *The Nazi State* (New York: Farrar, 1943) 132.

15. Frits von der Lippe, personal interview, 21 May 1981. Further von der Lippe quotations below are from this interview.

16. Svein Johs Ottesen, personal interview, 22 May 1981.

17. Kjell Larsgaard, letter to the author, 2 Oct. 1981.

18. Richard Petrow, *The Bitter Years: The Invasion and Occupation of Denmark and Norway, April 1940–May 1945* (New York: Morrow, 1974) 4–110.

19. John Steinbeck, *The Moon Is Down*, unrevised galley proofs (Austin: Harry Ransom Humanities Research Center, University of Texas).

20. Larsgaard, letter to the author.

21. Hølmebakk, personal interview.

22. Molaug, "Steinbeck-romanen om okkupasjonstiden" ["A Steinbeck Novel about the Occupation"], rev. of *Natt uten måne*, Fædrelandsvennen [Kristiansand] 23 July 1945: [3]. I am indebted to Eva Van Hooser for the English translation.

23. Ottesen, personal interview.

24. John Steinbeck, "The American Author John Steinbeck Sends This Greeting to Norway," *Bulletinen* May 1943: 7. I am grateful to Erling Grønland for the English translation.

25. Aas, letter to the author.

26. "*Natt uten måne*: John Steinbecks krigsroman med norsk motiv" ["*The Moon Is Down*: John Steinbeck's War Novel with a Norwegian Motif"], rev. of *Natt uten måne*, *Vestlandske Tidende* [Arendel] 3 July 1945: n. pag. The English translation is by Eva Van Hooser.

27. Corey Ford and Alastair MacBain, *Cloak and Dagger: The Secret Story of OSS* (New York: Random, 1945) 36–37. I have changed one detail of Ford and MacBain's account of Colby and his men parachuting into Norway. Ford and MacBain say it

took place on Easter Sunday; Colby insists it occurred on Palm Sunday (letter to the author, 27 May 1982).

28. William E. Colby, letter to the author, 30 Mar. 1981.

3. DENMARK

1. Mogens Staffeldt, personal interview, 20 May 1981.

2. David Lampe, *The Savage Canary: The Story of the Resistance in Denmark* (London: Cassell, 1957) 2, 36.

3. Jørgen Hæstrup, *Secret Alliance: A Study of the Danish Resistance Movement, 1940–45*, trans. Alison Borch-Johansen, 3 vols. ([Odense]: Odense University Press, 1976) 1: 15–16.

4. Lampe 2.

5. Jørgen Hæstrup, *From Occupied to Ally: Danish Resistance Movement, 1940–45*, trans. Reginald Spink (Copenhagen: Det Berlingske Bogtrykkeri, 1963) 8–11.

6. Jørgen Jacobsen, personal interview, 18 May 1981.

7. Jacobsen, personal interview.

8. Tetsumaro Hayashi, "Steinbeck's Political Vision in *The Moon Is Down*," *Steinbeck's World War II Fiction*, The Moon Is Down: *Three Explications*, Essay Series, No. 1 (Muncie, IN: Steinbeck Research Institute, Ball State University, 1986) 2.

9. Jørgen Jacobsen, letter to the author, 30 Oct. 1982.

10. Harold Flender, *Rescue in Denmark* (New York: Simon, 1963) 57–58.

11. Staffeldt, personal interview.

12. Staffeldt, personal interview.

13. Jacobsen, personal interview.

14. John Steinbeck, *The Moon Is Down* (New York: Viking, 1942) 178.

15. Mogens Knudsen, personal interview, 20 May 1981.

16. [Jacobsen, Jørgen, and Paul Lang], "Forlagets efterskrift," *Maanen er skjult*, [trans. Jørgen Jacobsen and Paul Lang] ([Copenhagen]: De Danske Studenters Forlag, [1942]) [59].

17. Hæstrup, *From Occupied to Ally* 27–31.

18. Flender 229.

19. Leo Buschardt, Albert Fabritius, and Helge Tønnesen, *Besættelsestidens illegale blade og bøger [Illegal Pamphlets and Books of the Period of Occupation]* (Copenhagen: Det Kongelige Bibliotek, 1954) 191–92, items 362–75. See also p. 8, item 463, in the *Supplement* to the above, and p. 7, items 574–83, in the typescript *Supplement II til Alfabetisk fortegnelse over illegale bøger [Second Supplement to the Alphabetical Index of Illegal Books]* ([Copenhagen]: [Det Kongelige Bibliotek], n.d.).

20. Knudsen, personal interview.

21. Flender 230–32; Staffeldt, personal interview.

4. HOLLAND

1. This and all subsequent quotations of Ferdinand Sterneberg are from a personal interview of 25 May 1981.

2. Steinbeck, *The Moon Is Down* 118–19.

3. Steinbeck, *The Moon Is Down* 185.

4. See also Anna E. C. Simoni, comp., *Publish and Be Free: A Catalogue of Clandestine Books Printed in the Netherlands, 1940–1945, in the British Library* (The Hague: Martinus Nijhoff, 1975) 187.

5. Goldstone and Payne, *Steinbeck* 154; *Index Translationum: International Bibliography of Translations*, vol. 30 (Paris: UNESCO, 1977) 577.

5. FRANCE

1. This discussion of the founding of the Éditions de Minuit and of its subsequent publications is taken from Jacques Debû-Bridel, *Les Éditions de Minuit: Historique et bibliographie* (Paris: Éditions de Minuit, 1945). I am indebted to Mary Gutermuth and Donald Stalling for the English translation.

2. This information comes from Pierre Rosselli, who helped his father, Jean-Pierre, a former member of the resistance, to arrange meetings for me with people who had worked with the Éditions de Minuit during the occupation. Early in May 1981 Pierre, then a student of journalism in Paris, telephoned Mme. Paraf-Desvignes (known at that time by the hyphenated combination of her married name, Motchane, and her old nom de guerre) to set up an appointment for me. During the course of that conversation, Mme. Motchane-Desvignes mentioned in passing that it was Eluard who had suggested the title *Nuits noires*. She then agreed to see me sometime between 17 May and 22 May and to

provide further information about her translation of Steinbeck's novel. Unfortunately, Mme. Motchane-Desvignes died suddenly a few days before I arrived in Paris to interview her.

3. Albert Gerard, *À la recontre de John Steinbeck [A Reassessment of John Steinbeck]* ([Brussels]: La Sixaine, [1947]) 30.

4. Jean-Paul Sartre, "American Novelists in French Eyes," *Atlantic Monthly* Aug. 1946: 116.

5. Yvonne Paraf-Desvignes, Note du traducteur, *Nuits noires* (Paris: Éditions de Minuit, 1944) [7].

6. *Nuits noires* [4].

6. OTHER COUNTRIES

1. Steinbeck, *Life in Letters* 590.

2. Bo Beskow, personal interview, 23 May 1981.

3. Steinbeck, *Life in Letters* 251.

4. Debû-Bridel, *Éditions de Minuit* 78.

5. For this discussion of Anna Katharina Rehmann-Salten and the publication and reception of her translation and dramatization of *The Moon Is Down* in Switzerland, I am indebted to her widower, Zürich lawyer Dr. Veit Wyler (letters to the author 17 Mar. 1982 and 2 Apr. 1982).

6. Heinrich Straumann, *American Literature in the Twentieth Century* (London: Hutchinson, 1951) 179, n.1.

7. Deming Brown, *Soviet Attitudes toward American Writing* (Princeton: Princeton University Press, 1962) 139.

8. Glenora W. Brown and Deming B. Brown, *A Guide to Soviet Russian Translations of American Literature,* Columbia Slavic Studies (New York: Columbia University, King's Crown, 1954) 195.

9. D. Brown 139, n. 5.

10. For this discussion of the translation and publication of *The Moon Is Down* in China I am indebted to Professor Chien Gochuen, letter to the author, 4 Sept. 1981, and to the Zhong Hua Book Company in Beijing, letter to the author, 22 Apr. 1981.

11. I am grateful to Ray Tsai and to another Zhong Hua Book Company—this one in Taipei—for supplying this translation.

7. CONCLUSION

1. Stanley Edgar Hyman, "Some Notes on John Steinbeck," *Antioch Review* June 1942, rpt. in *Steinbeck and His Critics*, ed. E. W. Tedlock, Jr., and C. V. Wicker (Albuquerque: University of New Mexico Press, 1957) 165.

2. Jean-Paul Sartre, *What Is Literature?* trans. Bernard Frechtman (New York: Philosophical, 1949) 70–73.

3. Roy S. Simmonds, "Steinbeck and World War II: The Moon Goes Down," *Steinbeck Quarterly* Winter–Spring 1984: 32.

4. Donald Weeks, "Steinbeck against Steinbeck," *Pacific Spectator* Autumn 1947, rpt. in *John Steinbeck*, ed. Harold Bloom (New York: Chelsea, 1987) 14.

5. Frederick J. Hoffman, *The Modern Novel in America, 1900–1950* (Chicago: Henry Regnery, 1951) 146.

6. John Ditsky, "Steinbeck's 'European' Play-Novella: *The Moon Is Down*," *Steinbeck Quarterly* Winter–Spring 1987, rpt. in *The Short Novels of John Steinbeck*, ed. Jackson J. Benson (Durham: Duke University Press, 1990) 108.

7. Benson, *True Adventures* 587.

8. Niccolo Machiavelli, *The Prince*, trans. George Bull (New York: Penguin, 1987) 47–49.

9. Edmund Wilson, *The Boys in the Back Room* (San Francisco: Colt, 1941) 41–53.

10. Steinbeck, *The Moon Is Down* 185–86.

11. Jackson J. Benson, "Through a Political Glass, Darkly: The Example of John Steinbeck," *Studies in American Fiction* Spring 1984: 54.

12. Straumann 109–10.

13. Simmonds 33.

14. Goldstone and Payne, *Steinbeck* 147–93; *Index Translationum*, vols. 25–36; Online Union Catalogue Database of OCLC (Online Computer Library Center).

15. Benson, *True Adventures* 498.

Works Cited

BOOKS

Benson, Jackson J. *Looking for Steinbeck's Ghost.* Norman: University of Oklahoma Press, 1988.

————. *The True Adventures of John Steinbeck, Writer.* New York: Viking, 1984.

Brown, Anthony Cave. *The Last Hero: Wild Bill Donovan.* New York: Times, 1982.

Brown, Deming. *Soviet Attitudes toward American Writing.* Princeton: Princeton University Press, 1962.

Brown, Glenora W., and Deming B. Brown. *A Guide to Soviet Russian Translations of American Literature.* Columbia Slavic Studies. New York: Columbia University, King's Crown, 1954.

Buschardt, Leo, Albert Fabritius, and Helge Tønnesen. *Besættelsestidens illegale blade og bøger [Illegal Pamphlets and Books of the Period of Occupation].* Copenhagen: Det Kongelige Bibliotek, 1954.

————. *Supplement og rettelser til besættelsestidens illegale blade og bøger [Supplement and Revisions to Illegal Pamphlets and*

Books of the Period of Occupation]. Copenhagen: Det Kongelige Bibliotek, 1954.

————. *Supplement II til Alfabetisk fortegnelse over illegale bøger [Second Supplement to the Alphabetical Index of Illegal Books]*. Typescript. [Copenhagen]: [Det Kongelige Bibliotek], n.d.

Debû-Bridel, Jacques. *Les Éditions de Minuit: Historique et bibliographie*. Paris: Éditions de Minuit, 1945.

Ebenstein, William. *The Nazi State*. New York: Farrar, 1943.

Flender, Harold. *Rescue in Denmark*. New York: Simon, 1963.

Ford, Corey, and Alastair MacBain. *Cloak and Dagger: The Secret Story of OSS*. New York: Random, 1945.

Gerard, Albert. *Á la recontre de John Steinbeck [A Reassessment of John Steinbeck]*. [Brussels]: La Sixaine, [1947].

Goldstone, Adrian H., and John R. Payne. *John Steinbeck: A Bibliographical Catalogue of the Adrian H. Goldstone Collection*. Austin: University of Texas Humanities Research Center, 1974.

Hæstrup, Jørgen. *From Occupied to Ally: Danish Resistance Movement, 1940–45*. Trans. Reginald Spink. Copenhagen: Det Berlingske Bogtrykkeri, 1963.

————. *Secret Alliance: A Study of the Danish Resistance Movement, 1940–45*. Trans. Alison Borch-Johansen. 3 vols. [Odense]: Odense University Press, 1976.

Hayashi, Tetsumaro. *Steinbeck's World War II Fiction*, The Moon Is Down: *Three Explications*. Essay Series, No. 1. Muncie, IN: Steinbeck Research Institute, Ball State University, 1986.

WORKS CITED

Hoffman, Frederick J. *The Modern Novel in America*, 1900–1950. Chicago: Henry Regnery, 1951.

Index Translationum: International Bibliography of Translations. Vols. 25–36. Paris: UNESCO, 1972–83.

Kiernan, Thomas. *The Intricate Music: A Biography of John Steinbeck*. Boston: Little, 1979.

Lampe, David. *The Savage Canary: The Story of the Resistance in Denmark*. London: Cassell, 1957.

Machiavelli, Niccolo. *The Prince*. Trans. George Bull. New York: Penguin, 1987.

Millichap, Joseph R. *Steinbeck and Film*. New York: Ungar, 1983.

Petrow, Richard. *The Bitter Years: The Invasion and Occupation of Denmark and Norway, April 1940–May 1945*. New York: Morrow, 1974.

Reynolds, Quentin. *The Curtain Rises*. New York: Random, 1944.

Sartre, Jean-Paul. *What Is Literature?* Trans. Bernard Frechtman. New York: Philosophical, 1949.

Simoni, Anna E. C., comp. *Publish and Be Free: A Catalogue of Clandestine Books Printed in the Netherlands, 1940–45, in the British Library*. The Hague: Martinus Nijhoff, 1975.

Steinbeck, John. *Maanen er gaaet ned* [*The Moon Is Down*]. N.p.: Frit Nordisk Forlag, 1943 [1944].

———. *Maanen er skjult* [*The Moon Is Down*]. [Trans. Jørgen Jacobsen and Paul Lang.] [Copenhagen]: De Danske Studenters Forlag, [1942].

———. *The Moon Is Down*. New York: Viking, 1942.

———. *The Moon Is Down*. Unrevised galley proofs. Austin: Harry Ransom Humanities Research Center, University of Texas.

———. *The Moon Is Down: Play in Two Parts*. London: English Theatre Guild, 1943.

———. *Natt uten måne* [*The Moon Is Down*]. Stockholm: Åhlén and Åkerlunds, 1942.

———. *Nuits noires* [*The Moon Is Down*]. [Trans. Yvonne Paraf.] Paris: Éditions de Minuit, 1944.

———. *Steinbeck: A Life in Letters*. Ed. Elaine Steinbeck and Robert Wallsten. New York: Viking, 1975.

———. *Die vliegenvanger* [*The Moon Is Down*]. Occupied Netherlands: [De Bizige Bij], 1944.

Straumann, Heinrich. *American Literature in the Twentieth Century*. London: Hutchinson, 1951.

Wilson, Edmund. *The Boys in the Back Room*. San Francisco: Colt, 1941.

Winkler, Allan M. *The Politics of Propaganda: The Office of War Information, 1942–1945*. New Haven: Yale University Press, 1978.

ARTICLES

Benson, Jackson J. "Through a Political Glass, Darkly: The Example of John Steinbeck." *Studies in American Fiction* Spring 1984: 45–59.

WORKS CITED

Best, Marshall A. Letter. *New Republic* 30 Mar. 1942: 431.

Chamberlain, John. "Books of the Times." Rev. of *The Moon Is Down*, by John Steinbeck. *New York Times* 6 Mar. 1942: 19.

Ditsky, John. "Steinbeck's 'European' Play-Novella: *The Moon Is Down*." *Steinbeck Quarterly* Winter–Spring 1987: 9–18. Rpt. in *The Short Novels of John Steinbeck*. Ed. Jackson J. Benson. Durham: Duke University Press, 1990. 101–10.

Duffus, R. L. "John Steinbeck's Heroic Tale '*The Moon Is Down*' Is a Narrative of Great Dramatic Intensity." Rev. of *The Moon Is Down*, by John Steinbeck. *New York Times Book Review* 8 Mar. 1942, sec. 6: 1, 27.

Fadiman, Clifton. "Steinbeck Again." Rev. of *The Moon Is Down*, by John Steinbeck. *New Yorker* 4 Apr. 1942: 63.

———. "Two Ways to Win the War." Rev. of *The Moon Is Down*, by John Steinbeck. *New Yorker* 7 Mar. 1942: 52–54.

French, Warren. "*The Moon Is Down*: John Steinbeck's 'Times.'" *Steinbeck Quarterly* Summer–Fall 1978: 77–87.

Gannett, Lewis. "Books and Things." *Herald Tribune* [New York] 4 May 1942: 11.

———. Introduction: "John Steinbeck's Way of Writing." *The Portable Steinbeck*. Ed. Pascal Covici. 1969 ed. New York: Viking, 1943. vii–xxviii.

Gunther, John. Rev. of *The Moon Is Down*, by John Steinbeck. *Herald Tribune Books* [New York] 8 Mar. 1942: 1.

Hyman, Stanley Edgar. "Some Notes on John Steinbeck." *Antioch Review* June 1942. Rpt. in *Steinbeck and His Critics*. Ed. E. W.

Tedlock, Jr., and C. V. Wicker. Albuquerque: University of New Mexico Press, 1957. 152–66.

[Jacobsen, Jørgen, and Paul Lang]. Forlagets efterskrift [Publisher's postscript]. *Mannen er skjult* [*The Moon Is Down*]. By John Steinbeck. [Trans. Jørgen Jacobsen and Paul Lang.] [Copenhagen]: De Danske Studenters Forlag, [1942].

Molaug. "Steinbeck-romanen om okkupasjonstiden" ["A Steinbeck Novel about the Occupation"]. Rev. of *Natt uten måne*, by John Steinbeck. *Fædrelandsvennen* [Kristiansand] 23 July 1945: n. pag.

"'The Moon Is Down': Steinbeck Extols Humanity at War." Rev. of *The Moon Is Down*, by John Steinbeck. *Life* 6 Apr. 1942: 32–33.

"The Moon Is Halfway Down." Editorial. *New Republic* 18 May 1942: 657.

"Mr. Steinbeck, Friends and Foes." Editorial. *New Republic* 30 Mar. 1942: 413.

"*Natt uten måne*: John Steinbecks krigsroman med norsk motiv" ["*The Moon Is Down*: John Steinbeck's War Novel with a Norwegian Motif"]. Rev. of *Natt uten måne*, by John Steinbeck. *Vestlandske Tidende* [Arendal] 3 July 1945: n. pag.

Nelson, Frank G. Letter. *New Republic* 13 Apr. 1942: 495.

"Notes on Books and Authors," *New York Times* 28 Apr. 1942: 19.

Olav, Hans. Letter. *New Republic* 4 May 1942: 607–08.

WORKS CITED

Paraf-Desvignes, Yvonne. Note du traducteur. [Translator's Note]. *Nuits noires*. By John Steinbeck. Paris: Éditions de Minuit, 1944. [7].

"Polish Refugee." Letter. *New Republic* 30 Mar. 1942: 431–32.

Sartre, Jean-Paul. "American Novelists in French Eyes." *Atlantic Monthly* Aug. 1946: 114–18.

Schulberg, Budd. "John Steinbeck: A Lion in Winter." *The Four Seasons of Success*. Garden City, NY: Doubleday, 1972. 187–97. Rpt. in *Conversations with John Steinbeck*. Ed. Thomas Fensch. Jackson: University Press of Mississippi, 1988. 105–12.

Simmonds, Roy S. "Steinbeck and World War II: The Moon Goes Down." *Steinbeck Quarterly* Winter–Spring 1984: 14–34.

Steinbeck, John. "About Ed Ricketts." *The Log from the Sea of Cortez*. By John Steinbeck and Ed Ricketts. New York: Viking, 1951. vii–lxvii.

———. "The American Author John Steinbeck Sends This Greeting to Norway." *Bulletinen* May 1943: 7.

———. Forlagets efterskrift [Publisher's postscript]. *Maanen er gaaet ned* [*The Moon Is Down*]. By John Steinbeck. N.p.: Frit Nordisk Forlag, 1943 [1944]. [70].

———. "Letters to Alicia." *Weekend with Newsday* 11 Dec. 1965: 3W.

———. "My Short Novels." *Steinbeck and His Critics*. Ed. E. W. Tedlock, Jr., and C. V. Wicker. Albuquerque: University of New Mexico Press, 1957. 38–40.

———. "Reflections on a Lunar Eclipse." *Herald Tribune* [New York] 6 Oct. 1963, Sunday *Book Week* section: 3.

———. "The Secret Weapon We Were Afraid to Use." *Colliers* 10 Jan. 1953: 9–13.

Thurber, James. Letter. *New Republic* 30 Mar. 1942: 431.

———. "What Price Conquest?" Rev. of *The Moon Is Down*, by John Steinbeck. *New Republic* 16 Mar. 1942: 370.

"Viewpoint of Victory." Rev. of *The Moon Is Down*, by John Steinbeck. *Time* 9 Mar. 1942: 84–88.

Weeks, Donald. "Steinbeck against Steinbeck." *Pacific Spectator* Autumn 1947. Rpt. in *John Steinbeck*. Ed. Harold Bloom. New York: Chelsea, 1987. 7–18.

LETTERS TO THE AUTHOR

Aas, Oddvar. 18 July 1981.

Chien, Gochuen. 4 Sept. 1981.

Colby, William E. 30 Mar. 1981 and 27 May 1982.

Dunlop, Richard. 31 Mar. 1981.

Helms, Richard. 23 Mar. 1981.

Jacobsen, Jørgen. 30 Oct. 1982.

Larsgaard, Kjell. 2 Oct. 1981.

MacLeish, Archibald. 8 Apr. 1981.

Roosevelt, Kermit. 20 Mar. 1981.

Skouen, Arne. 10 Aug. 1981.

WORKS CITED

Steinbeck, Elaine. 1 Nov. 1979.

Strawderman, Larry R. (response to a Freedom of Information Act request). 20 July 1982.

Troy, Thomas F. 20 Jan. 1982.

Wyler, Veit. 17 Mar. 1982 and 2 Apr. 1982.

Zhong Hua Company in Beijing. 22 Apr. 1981.

PERSONAL INTERVIEWS

Beskow, Bo. 23 May 1981.

Dahl, John. 22 May 1981.

Hølmebakk, Gordon. 21 May 1981.

Jacobsen, Jørgen. 18 May 1981.

Knudsen, Mogens. 20 May 1981.

Ottesen, Svein Johs. 22 May 1981.

Rosselli, Pierre. 16 May 1981.

Staffeldt, Mogens. 20 May 1981.

Sterneberg, Ferdinand. 25 May 1981.

Von der Lippe, Frits. 21 May 1981.

COMPUTER SERVICE

Online Catalogue Database of the OCLC (Online Computer Library Center).

Index

INDEX

INDEX